A Doctor's Experiences of Life

A Doctor's Experiences of Life

by

Patrick Dignan

The Pentland Press Limited
Edinburgh · Cambridge · Durham

First published in 1994 by
The Pentland Press Ltd.
1 Hutton Close
South Church
Bishop Auckland
Durham

ISBN 1 85821 136 0

Typeset by Elite Typesetting Techniques, Southampton.
Printed and bound by Antony Rowe Ltd., Chippenham.

To the Royal Army Medical Corps
and to the former Director General Army
Medical Services, the Late Lieutenant
General Sir Alexander Drummond KBE CB

Contents

Illustrations

Foreword

by Colonel TAI Bouchier Hayes

The Irish are a very fair race. They never speak well of each other, so it was with some amazement that I received the invitation from Patrick Dignan to write the foreword to his autobiography. He was taking a chance in asking another Irishman, member of the RAMC and a general practitioner to boot, but he must have suspected my unexpressed admiration and affection.

His book is a delight, written in a very simple style which captures the caring attitude of a completely uncynical gentleman. The trademarks of Patrick's life have always been common sense and uncommon sensibility, his view that there were advantages in working in general practice before embarking on a surgical career being music to my ears. In the RAMC all doctors must spend at least one year as a Regimental Medical Officer before undertaking any specialist training. This experience creates an atmosphere in which hospital specialists understand the myriad problems that the general practitioner faces and is sympathetic to them. The patient benefits are great because of this enhancement at the GP Hospital interface. Nothing in medicine has given me more satisfaction, and it is the cornerstone of high morale in the RAMC.

The Devil is said to have all the best songs, but Patrick has a large fund of excellent stories which have deliberately been omitted in this book. Patrick would never tell a story that reflected badly on anybody other than himself, and he would never cause any hurt or commit any offence, even humorously. No names, no packdrill is another of his mottoes.

One story tells more about Patrick than any other. As a Regimental Medical Officer I had an army car at my disposal, but Patrick as a mere General was expected to make his own way to work. A Guards Officer called Rupert joined us on our way to work. I introduced Rupert to the General. 'Rupert, this is General Dignan'. Rupert misheard me and replied 'Good morning Gerald'. Because we were working in London none of us were in uniform. It would never have occurred to Patrick to correct the officer's greeting and, from then on, every morning the greeting was repeated.

The day eventually came when 'Gerald' the General was in uniform. Rupert fell back in the car in great embarrassment. The General was even more embarrassed because of Rupert's distress. There was not a word said to me by Patrick about my perverse sense of humour, displayed when I failed to correct Rupert's greeting at the time he first met Patrick. What was London Transport's gain was our loss, as Rupert subsequently never travelled with us again.

What a patient expects of a good doctor in order of priority are availability, amiability and ability. These characteristics were never better demonstrated than when my son was ill at home with abdominal pain. I asked Patrick for his medical opinion each morning and evening and for five days he visited and examined Tommy.

The outcome was a double success. Tommy got better, and cynical youth found a role model of a caring, generous and considerate man whom he attempted to emulate.

The Dignans are a wonderfully cohesive family, full of humour, charm and success. Each of the children has made a great personal success of life. This does not happen by accident, but as the result of a caring and considerate Christian background. The highest tribute that I can pay to Patrick is that he is of the same mould as another great man – my father.

Ask not where my glory begins or ends.

But say my glory was, I had such friends.

T A I BOUCHIER HAYES

Chapter 1

Introduction

Shortly after my seventieth birthday I retired, and my career in the practice of medicine abruptly ended. When I looked back, I realised that I had been engaged in the practice of my profession for nearly half a century.

When my wife, Eileen, asked me how I felt being retired, I told her I felt I was in limbo, and quoted the Oxford Dictionary's meaning of the word, limbo, 'a place in which forgotten or unwanted things collect'.

Looking back, I found I had more to reflect on than Captain Boyle, a character in one of Sean O'Casey's plays. In the play, Joxer Daly, a cronie of Captain Boyle, encourages the good Captain to reflect upon his earlier life, when he says to him, 'God be with the young days, when you were steppen the deck of a manly ship, with the win blowin a hurricane through the masts, an the only sound you'd hear was "Port your helm", and the only answer, "Port it is sir".'

Captain Boyle in reply says, 'Them was days, Joxer, them was days. Sailin from the Gulf o Mexico to the Antarctic Ocean I seen things, I seen things Joxer, that no mortal man should speak about that know his catechism. Often an often, when I was on the wheel with a marlin spike, an the win's blowing fierce an the waves lashin and lashin, till you'd think every minute goin to be your last, an it blowed and blowed – blew is the right word Joxer – but blowed is what the sailors use.' Joxer interjects, saying, 'Aw it is a darlin word, a darlin word.' The Captain continues with his reflections and says, 'As it blowed an blowed, I often looked up at the sky an ass meself the question, what is the stars, what is the stars, an then I'd have another look, an I'd ass meself, what is the moon?' Earlier in the play, his wife, when they are arguing with each other, says to him, 'Everybody callin you Captain, an you only waint on the water, in a collier from here to Liverpool, when anybody to look listen or look at you, wud take you for a second Christo For Colombus!'

In reporting my experiences, unlike the good Captain, I have endeavoured not to embellish fact with fiction.

My Childhood

My surname is an anglicised form of the Irish name, O'Duigenan. My father was born in the West of Ireland, where his ancestors came from. During the sixteenth and seventeenth centuries, the O'Duigenans were one of the more important literary families in Ireland. They were bards and teachers to the leading clans in the country.

The motto on their Coat of Arms was 'Historia Magistra Vitae'. The most noted ancester was one of the Four Masters. The Four Masters compiled the *Annals of the Kingdom of Ireland*, a history of Ireland from the earliest times to 1616. The literary tradition, later on, was perpetuated by Doctor Patrick Duigenan (1735-1861), who was a notable polemical in his day, and a Fellow of Trinity College, Dublin. In the Military sphere, the names of the Duigenans, can be found amongst the officers of King James II's Irish Army.

My mother, on the other hand, was born in Protestant Northern Ireland. Her family had a very large residence and farm there. She had aristocratic ancestors, her great-great-grandfather being a duke.

My father served in the First World War in the Artists Rifles, the forerunner of the present day Volunteer SAS. During his service, he was seconded to the War Office, where he performed the duties of collating the daily list of war casualties, which he subsequently regularly presented to the War Minister in the Houses of Parliament. Sadly, one of his experiences was the sight of the names of his two brothers on the list of casualties. They had been killed at the Battle of the Somme. On the brighter side, from his experiences of attending the House of Commons, he became a good raconteur of extracts taken from speeches delivered by famous MPs. In later life, he would quote some of them to me, and one I well remember was 'You are over exacerbated by the exuberance of your own verbosity and you are a heterogeneous humbug.'

After the War, he returned to Ireland, and set up a home with my mother in Dublin. Soon after he returned, he was subjected to the humiliation of being arrested by the Black and Tans, as a result of being an innocent bystander at the scene of the murder of one of their officers. He was, however, released from their custody, after he had given proof of his identity. He was awarded a post-war University grant to study for a degree in Agriculture. Unfortunately, he found it difficult to settle down and, subsequently, did not take up farming as a career. Eventually, he established himself as a House Property Agent.

My parents had nine sons but no daughters. Four of my brothers died in infancy or early childhood.

I went to a Christian Brothers school in Dublin. The *espirit de corps* in the school was founded on hard work in the classroom and indeed on the playing fields. It was engendered by strong discipline, which to some extent was enforced by the use of the strap. Fortunately, I found at an early stage that I had an exceptionally good talent for playing games, especially Gaelic football. As time went on, I used that talent to help me gain immunity to the strap, by working hard on the perfection of my playing ability, and as a result, becoming an indispensable member of our school team. Like our modern day 'prima donnas' in professional football, I became rather temperamental, and had to be treated with respect on and off the playing field, and indeed, in the classroom. There were two incidental factors involved in my fitness training. One concerned my serving at seven o'clock Mass, which, because I was a late riser, entailed running about a mile to church each morning. The other factor involved a greyhound my father had been given. I had to take the dog for runs on a strand and walks on a canal bank. Regrettably, from my point of view, he, was infinitely more successful in the races he ran than I was in the field of athletics.

My footballing career, however, ended up with a flourish of, what my team mates, felt was heroic endeavour. In my last game, the final of our Colleges championship, our coach, before the match, gave me some specific instructions. They were, in effect, to mark our opponents star player very closely. Soon after the match started, I jumped with him, contesting a high ball, As I did so, I regrettably and, I hasten to add, accidentally, made violent contact with him. From then on, he was unable to take part in the game effectively. We subsequently won the match comfortably.

In addition to our physical activities on the playing fields, we also had to take part in a short period of physical training exercises in the school yard each morning before the commencement of our classes.

There was also a cultural aspect to our extra-curriculum activities, namely the annual production of an opera. As a result of this activity, a love of the music of the opera was engendered in me, and it has remained with me ever since.

In closing this chapter on my schoolboy days, I look back with admiration for the Christian Brothers. They gave me a sound education, and

'Jumping for the ball'.

instilled in me a sense of good self-discipline, moral obligation and behaviour.

Having been awarded an Honours School Leaving Certificate in 1937, I became eligible to enter a university in Dublin. My father, at that time felt, that, because of Hitler's aims of expanding Germany's power in Europe, and perhaps in the World, another Great War was inevitable, sooner or later. From his experiences of working in the War Office in the last war, and being involved in collating the casualty figures, and from the tragic loss of his own two brothers in that war, he developed a deep-seated abhorrence of war. As a consequence, he became determined that the lives of his five sons should not be at risk fighting in a war. He advised and encouraged us all to study Medicine, not only because it was a noble profession, but also, because, it would ensure us a non-combatant role in a future war. He also decided that we should enter Trinity College, a Protestant University, because of its great traditions, and its world-wide standing as a seat of learning.

Chapter 2

My Years at Medical School

I entered the Medical School of Trinity College, Dublin at the age of seventeen years. At that time, Roman Catholics were excommunicated if they entered Trinity without special dispensation from the Archbishop of Dublin. At my next confession, I informed the priest, a monk, that I had doubts about my father having obtained the necessary dispensation. To my amazement, the priest remarked that it was a great university, and expressed the wish he had gone to it himself. I remember, when I attended the Registrar's Office on my first day at the Medical School, to complete the necessary documentation, a Nigerian student in front of me was being requested to record his religion on his Entrance Form. The student did not have a religion to record. The Registrar read out a list of various religions to him, and then suggested that he choose the Protestant one, on the grounds that it seemed to be the most popular one in the University at that time. However, I am pleased to say that I never encountered any religious bigotry during the time I spent at University and, indeed, at no time was religion ever a subject for discussion amongst my fellow students. It is nice to know that, some years later, the ban was removed, and, subsequently, large numbers of Catholics entered the University.

Some of our students were rather high-spirited. I remember the occasion when they lifted a Professor's Austin Seven car from outside a classroom building and deposited it on his desk in the lecture theatre. Incidentally, that Professor was usually late in starting his lecture. Invariably, a technician from his laboratory would apologise for his late arrival, by saying that he was engaged in some urgent work in the laboratory. On this occasion, the sight of the car on the Professor's desk startled the technician so much that, in uttering the apology, he stated that the Professor was finishing urgent work in the lavatory!

6

In our Medical School we had a unique body of medical students. They were referred to as chronic medical students. They were students who kept failing their examinations. They came from well-off families who could afford to keep them at university with no financial restraints and, as a result, they lacked incentive and motivation to study hard to pass their examinations and give up the good life they were enjoying as medical students. A few became legendary. Many anecdotes relating to their attempts to pass their examinations were recorded in the College folklore. At an Anatomy examination one of them was handed a femur (thigh bone), and in a vain attempt to pass the student and not have to confront him again at the examination, the examiner asked him a simple question, namely, how many of these bones did he have? The student replied that he had four! When asked how he could possibly have four, he stated that apart from his own two, and the one he held in his hand, he also had one back in his 'digs', which was part of a skeleton he used for learning his anatomy. When then asked which side of a body did the bone come from, he refused to attempt to answer the question, on the grounds that he wasn't 'up for honours'. Another student was shown a skull and when asked what went through the large opening in its base, replied with great aplomb, 'Many a good pint of stout, sir!'

These students were involved in many escapades, one of which I remember very well. Outside the front entrance to our College, the traffic was usually very busy, because of the inverted 'Y' traffic junction that was there. One day, during a peak lunch-time hour of traffic, a combined party of our medical students and engineering students approached the policeman on point duty, and informed him that they were from the Traffic Department of the Dublin Corporation. They then proceeded, whilst the policeman held up the traffic, to take 'sightings' and measure the widths of the traffic lanes. They took some considerable time doing their 'thing', and as a result, the biggest hold up of traffic that was ever seen in the City of Dublin developed!

Sadly, to relate from the point of view of the chronic medical students, soon after the appointment of a new Dean of the Medical School, an edict was circulated to all students, which stated that in future if a student failed to pass any examination after three attempts, he would be requested to leave the Medical School. It is of much interest that at about the time this edict was published, World War II broke out and many of the students who had to leave the School went to England and joined the armed services. As a postscript, it gives me great pleasure to record that many of them served throughout the War with great distinction.

Incidentally, in parallel with our medical studies, we also had to study for a Bachelor of Arts degree, and the acquisition of this degree before one qualified in Medicine was mandatory. My subjects for the degree were English Literature and Logic. Trinity College was unique in this respect. It required its students to have reached a standard of proficiency in certain modalities of learning, designed as an intellectual performance, before they could take their own particular academic degree.

Many years later, when I was watching the British Open Golf Championship on TV, my study of logic gave me food for thought. The commentator, when a player hit his ball into a bunker, remarked that the player 'wouldn't like that'. It then occurred to me that the logic of that remark meant that there must be some other players that would like it, i.e., being in the bunker, and consequently, Sunday morning golf club players, finding their ball in a bunker, might well jump up and down with joy, shouting 'I like it. I like it'!

As my first two years at Medical School progressed, I found that there was a fellow student who was extremely clever and able, and who was always top of the class, so to speak. Although not as clever as he was, I worked hard in my endeavours to compete with him in our examinations. I believe that it was a consequence of those endeavours that enabled me to emulate his achievements of being awarded a Medical Scholarship, a Demonstratorship in Anatomy and Physiology and share with him the Professor of Physiology Prize. In addition, we both passed the Primary FRCS examination. I was also appointed a part-time lecturer in Anatomy in the Apothecarys Hall. Looking back, I feel that these achievements were the launching pad for my career in medicine. At this early stage in my career, I found that of all the various fields in medicine, surgery interested me most. I felt that surgery was an exact science and required some of the skills that I acquired demonstrating anatomy.

Having completed my first two years at Medical School, learning the basic sciences of medicine, I spent the remaining three years of my training as a student in hospitals. I recall that early in this part of my career as a medical student, I served as a surgical dresser in a Casualty Department. It was then that I first became involved in the treatment of gunshot wounds. One morning, shortly after I arrived on duty, casualties from a gun battle involving policemen and IRA gunmen, were brought into the Department. Apparently, the British Ambassador's car carrying mail to the docks for shipment to England, and escorted by the police, was ambushed by the IRA. In the ensuing gun battle a policeman and an IRA gunman were seriously wounded. My involvement in the management of the casualties was to, immediately, at the request of the casualty officer who was aware of my blood group being that of a universal donor, donate a pint of blood to the most seriously wounded, the IRA gunman. Incidentally, many years later, when I was being security vetted in the Army, the vetting officer was very friendly and courteous until, in answer to a question, I admitted that I had an association with the IRA in the past. However, I quickly added that my link with them was purely haematic!

Mention of the Casualty Department, reminds me of the ingenuity displayed by the Casualty Officer in his efforts to cope with the very long queue of patients waiting to be seen every evening. Many of these patients suffered from minor and inconsequential complaints. The Casualty Officer would walk down the length of the queue, and wearing a blood-stained apron and carrying a large plaster shears, he would shout loudly, 'Anyone for removal of a plaster?' As a result, the patients would become somewhat scared, and those with trivial complaints would depart hurriedly from the Department!

During the time I spent in the opening theatre, there was a surgeon I recall, who warranted the pseudonym of 'blood and thunder' because of the amount of blood he spilt during an operation, and the loud rumbling noise he made when a student didn't carry out his instructions correctly when assisting him. I hasten to add, however, he was nonetheless a very good surgeon. There was a surgeon in another hospital, who on one hand treated his students with kindness and civility, but on the other hand had no time for students who came from other hospitals. He referred to the latter students as being foreign students! I remember one dark winter's morning when I attended his ward round. There was no bulb in the light socket above the head of the bed of the patient he was going to examine and discuss with us. I was in the process of displaying my initiative and impress him, by taking a bulb from above the bed of another patient, when the surgeon placed his hand on my shoulder and told me that, since I was not a student of his hospital, I had no right to do what I was doing. I somehow or other, and rightly or wrongly, got the impression from his attitude that I was *persona non grata* on his ward round. Needless to say, I didn't reappear again on his ward round.

My first insight into the effects of war may have on a person presented to me when a surgeon returned to work in his hospital after he had been serving in the Army that had been evacuated from Dunkirk. He would appear in the hospital very early in the morning and arrange for his operating list to commence, much to the discomfort of all concerned with it. My feeling, looking back now, was that he was suffering from 'emotional shock' or what, nowadays, is called 'Post Traumatic Stress'.

A physician had a patient who suffered from a rare condition, called Porphyria. One of the characteristics of this condition is that the urine of patients suffering from it becomes dark red in colour when exposed to daylight for sometime. This patient, being the only patient in Dublin who could produce such a unique specimen of urine, became a permanent resident in the hospital. His proud possessor, the physician, as a result, had his urine always 'on tap' for use in teaching his students, and for distribution to other teaching hospitals. The patient, I hasten to add, suffered from an incurable disease, and being poor, was pleased to get free board and lodgings in return for the use that was being made of his urine!

Another oddity was an elderly surgeon, whose fame arose from his propensity for removing, expertly, stones from the urinary tract. He used to carry a very large bladder stone around with him in the pocket of his white coat and produce if for identification by students he met in the corridors of the hospital.

A dermatologist had an unusual phobia – he could not stand the sight of a door being left open. His initial remark to any patient or member of staff entering his office would always be, 'Shut the door.'

During the time I spent learning how to deliver babies, I gained first-hand experience of what it is like living in the slums of a city. After spending some time in the maternity hospital, the student would then become eligible to go out on the district. It was not unusual to find the delivery taking place in the one room where all the family lived and where sanitation and washing facilities were poor. Usually, the student embarking on his first case outside the hospital would be accompanied by an experienced and more mature student. Living conditions were so good in the hospital that some students continued to work there, even though they had completed the number of deliveries they were required to perform. One such student, who because of the experience he had gained was treated with awe and great respect, accompanied me on my first visit to the district. Having examined the mother, he left me with the midwife to get on with the delivery whilst he, having been given a glass of whisky by the father in a room downstairs, promptly fell asleep. Some time later, I woke him up and informed him that our lady upstairs had just been delivered of twins. He remonstrated with me for not requesting his assistance in what he felt might have been a difficult case. Apparently, the delivery of twins in the district was a rare event, and to him, it would be like a golfer having a hole in one! As we cycled back to the hospital he appeared to be worried about losing face with the other students for not diagnosing the presence of twins and being involved in their delivery.

There was a pub near the hospital. The porter answering the enquiries about the whereabouts of a student who happened to be in the pub at the time, would say he was at a PPH, the initials for a post partum haemorrhage, but also for 'pub past the hospital'. Incidentally, the police were kind enough, from their point of view, to regard the pub as a no go area! However, one night a policeman new to the beat, and suspecting drinking on the premises after hours, demanded entrance to the pub. He found a number of students drinking pints of Guinness. He informed them that they were breaking the law and started taking down their names and addresses. When he asked one of the students, 'What's yours?' he replied, 'I'll have a pint.' At that moment he remembered being told by his station superior officer not to enter the premises, and to retrieve the situation, he removed his helmet and said, 'I'll have the same.'

Our summer holidays were long. I spent some of the time in the West of Ireland, helping my uncle on his farm. In return for my labour, he would arrange for me to fish, as often as possible, on a beautiful lake for perch and pike. I would also help my aunt, who lived not far away from my uncle, with the painting and decorating of her house and with her gardening. She was a top-class golfer and used to give me golf lessons. It was she who introduced me to the game.

On occasions, during the summer, I would fish off the coast near the entrance to Dun Laoghaire harbour with some friends. On one occasion we were all lying down in the boat, basking in the sun, when we were suddenly alerted by the noise of an aircraft. Looking up, to our horror and amazement, we saw a German plane descending on the Holyhead to Dublin mail steamer. The ship was only a few hundred yards away from us, and steaming in our direction. We just had enough time to steer our boat away from the ship and, fortunately, were not overturned by the wash produced by the ship. Meanwhile, the German aircraft had zoomed over the ship without attacking it and had flown away. When we came ashore and related our experience to some of the locals in a pub in Dun Laoghaire, they told us it was not unusual for a German aircraft to fly over the Irish mailboat during its voyage to Dublin. It was felt that these unfriendly acts were meant to intimidate our people and frighten them into remaining neutral in the War, although, in fact, Eire did not have the means or resources to fight with the Allies against the Germans, or indeed to defend itself against an enemy. However, a large number of Irishmen crossed the water and joined the British Army and, as far as I know, won more VCs than did servicemen from other countries.

My days spent as a medical student came to an end in June 1943, when I qualified as a doctor.

Chapter 3

My Time in General Practice

After I qualified, my ambition was to commence training for a career in surgery. However, I felt that before I did that I should help out with my family finances. In those days, there was no such thing as a grant being given to a student attending a university. In addition to my university fees, my father had the financial burden of my two elder brothers qualifying in medicine and was preparing for my two younger brothers to enter the medical school. The salary of an assistant to a general practitioner was ten pounds a week. On the other hand, a doctor working in a hospital as a house surgeon could be paid as little as one pound a week.

I found employment as an assistant to a GP in Essex in August 1943. I soon found that there were advantages, other than financial, in working in a general practice before embarking on my surgical career. To begin with, the experience one gained was in a broad field of medicine in general, including the primary care of the very young and the very old, and in their homes, the chronic sick and the dying. It also allowed one to get to know something about the environment the patient lived and worked in, and about his or her social background, including the stress factors that were involved in their illness and their recovery from it. In addition, it afforded one the opportunity to develop good skills in the art of communication with patients and their relatives.

I lived in my principal's very charming and comfortable house. We had a full-time resident housekeeper, who looked after us very well. My principal's wife and family lived in Ireland and, from time to time, he went there to visit them. He was very interested in horse-racing and attended race meetings at Newmarket. He had horses which he kept on the Essex marshes and I was expected to assist him with their feeding! He was also a member of a high-class club in London, which he visited fairly often. As a result of these activities of his, I was left in charge of the practice quite frequently, and this engendered in me a good sense of responsibility.

Fortunately, our practice was not very busy and it was possible to devote as much time as was necessary to see and treat our patients.

An interesting and valuable aspect to our work in the practice was the small pharmacy we had, and from which we dispensed standard prescriptions for common complaints, such as headaches, colds, coughs, and indigestion, etc.

I was also on call to deal with emergency cases on ships in the Thames Estuary. I remember being called to a Dutch ship on the morning of D-Day to see a case of appendicitis. The ship's captain took me to his cabin and handed me a glass of schnapps, which he said was in celebration of the news of the landing of the Allies on the beaches of Normandy, which he had just picked up on the ship's radio.

Incidentally, on the previous night there was strict security in the vicinity of a US Army camp, situated not far from our town, and as I took a short cut on the way to a maternity case, and passed close to the camp, I was stopped by the police. I had no means of identification on me. The police, I suspect because of my strong Irish accent, took a lot to convince them that indeed I was a doctor out on a call. They escorted me into the American Army camp, where I was interviewed by an officer, who had forebears who came from Ireland, and who after a brief discussion about my identity, let me go on my way. The police then allowed me to proceed on my journey but, however, followed me to the house I was visiting, where they sought confirmation of my identity from the husband of my patient.

In my extra-curriculum activities I was involved in two 'blackout' incidents. One occurred when I had a night out in London with my brother, who was a GP, and some other GPs. It was the first time I had drunk alcohol. I only drank two pints of Guinness. Nevertheless, having got on the Underground Circle line at 10.00 p.m. at the beginning of my journey back to Essex, I subsequently 'blacked out' and fell asleep. I woke up, I seem to remember, at Paddingston Station about three hours later. A very kind porter informed me that the train was being put away somewhere for the night. He got me a taxi and I stayed the night with my brother, who had his practice in London. The other incident occurred when I was walking in the 'blackout' in London. I collided with another pedestrian. We apologised to each other and, to my astonishment, the person I had bumped into was one of the surgeons who worked in a hospital, in Dublin, I had attended as a medical student. The chances of this incident occurring must have been more than a million to one.

My social life consisted mainly of visits to our local cinema, which happened to be conveniently located close to the surgery. I saw enough films to last me the rest of my life! Another aspect of my social life was my attendance at candlelight dinners my principal provided for his special guests, who were sometimes American Army officers he brought back from the races at Newmarket. We dined well in spite of the wartime rationing, thanks to the good nature of some of our patients, who were well-to-do farmers. They provided us with farm produce in abundance.

The war appeared to be very far away from us and the community we lived in, apart from the occasional sight of a flying bomb in the sky making its way to a target in London, having eluded the anti-aircraft defences. I, incidentally, had the experience of one of those bombs dropping on a main line station soon after I passed it as I drove through London.

My year spent in general practice was a very enjoyable and worthwhile experience. I strongly recommend working in general practice as essential basic training to be undertaken by all young doctors before they embark on training as specialists.

Before returning to Ireland, I spent a further brief period in general practice as a locum in Kent. After returning to Ireland, I found I had some time to spare before taking up a hospital surgical training appointment. I consequently spent two weeks as a locum in general practice in a small country town. On my first Sunday in the practice, I met three of the town's dignitaries after Mass, and they invited me to join them in a game of poker that evening. After the game, I found that I had lost what amounted to the fee I was being paid for doing the locum. However, little did I realise how soon I was going to recoup my losses!

At the beginning of my second week working in the practice, I was called to a manor where an Earl, who lived there, had suddenly become ill. When I arrived at the manor, the door was opened by a butler, who looked down at the bicycle clips I was wearing with some disdain – I had cycled there – and with disbelief, that wearing them, I could be the doctor. After examining the patient, I came to the conclusion that he had had a stroke, the most likely cause of which was a brain haemorrhage. I gave him an injection of morphine. During my discussion with her Ladyship about his condition, I got the impression that she wanted him to be seen by a specialist. I recalled the name of a Professor of Medicine and eventually contacted him at a race meeting just outside Dublin. He came straight away to see my patient and duly arrived at the manor driving a Rolls Royce. Having examined the patient, he informed me that the diagnosis was a brain thrombosis but, however, since the treatment of both conditions was similar and, in order to save face with her Ladyship, he felt that we should stick to my diagnosis. After he had discussed her husband's condition with her, he informed her Ladyship how very fortunate she was having such a good young doctor looking after him. Later, when he was leaving, he looked at my bicycle with some horror and amazement and told me that riding a bicycle to visit the patient would create a bad impression. In future, I was to hire a taxi.

By the end of the week my patient was much better, and, I was better off financially, having had a private patient to look after! In due course, the doctor I had been doing the locum for arrived back from his holiday. At first, he was profuse in his thanks for the work I had done on his behalf in the practice. However, on hearing about the illustrious private patient I had been treating, his attitude changed, and he gave me to understand, in no uncertain terms, that I should have phoned him about the patient's illness and if I had done so, he would have returned immediately from his holiday.

Chapter 4

Early Surgical Training

I spent the next six months as a surgical houseman in a Dublin teaching hospital. My memory of this time in my life revolves mainly around the elderly surgeon in charge of the unit I worked in. He was very kind and considerate and had a great depth of surgical experience and knowledge but however, was somewhat absent-minded. He taught me to use sound common sense, and to first consider the commonest causes of a condition when making a diagnosis. His clinical acumen was exceptional and is highlighted in the following anecdote. In the front hall of the hospital there were statuettes of famous pioneers in medicine. One of them was a forebear of the surgeon. One night, during a students' party, some students took that particular statuette to their rooms. Unfortunately, when later they were taking it back to its pedestal, they dropped it and broke it! They replaced it with a similar but somewhat smaller one they found somewhere else in the hospital. The next morning, after the surgeon had passed through the hall, he stopped and, turning to me, remarked that there was something out of place in the hall. Not wanting to be involved in the aftermath of the unfortunate incident of the previous night, I quickly diverted his attention to a patient who was being wheeled on a trolley into a nearby minor operating theatre. I knew something about this case. It was a very interesting case. The patient had a swelling behind his knee, which a young surgeon was about to open, thinking it was an abscess. My chief, having examined the swelling, turned his attention again to what he had observed to be out of place in the front hall, and began to make his way back to the hall. Once more, I attempted to divert his attention by asking him what he thought of the swelling. His response was to immediately rush back to the theatre. He arrived there just in time to stop the surgeon incising the swelling. He announced to us all, and to our amazement, that

17

the swelling was in fact an aneurysm! (an abnormal dilitation of an artery), which of course, meant, that cutting into the swelling would have caused a severe haemorrhage. The artery involved was the main artery in the patient's leg, and it occurred to me, that, if the students hadn't broken the statuette, the patient would almost certainly have lost his leg.

After I left the hospital in Dublin in August 1945, I journeyed by train to Belfast, to take up an appointment of Resident Surgical Officer in a large teaching hospital there. Upon my arrival at the main station in Belfast, my attention was drawn to the graffiti on its walls, which was in very large letters, and of anti-Popish nature, for example, 'To hell with the Pope'.

There were two main hospitals in Belfast. The one I was going to was, in those days, considered to be Protestant and other, Catholic. I soon got the impression that my appointment was based on the assumption that, being a graduate of Trinity College, I must be of the Protestant faith. However, not long after I had assumed the appointment, I began to feel I was being treated as if I was an outsider of some sort, and I began to wonder if it had become generally known that I was a Roman Catholic. This situation came to a head one morning when, at the end of a ward round, coffee was being served to the consultant and his staff in sister's office. The sister, in a fairly loud voice, asked me if I was Roman Catholic. When I replied that I was, she remarked, I seem to recall, 'So now we know', and shook my hand and welcomed me to the hospital. Incidentally, she and I subsequently got on very well together, and when I was leaving the hospital, presented me with a farewell present of a book. To return to the incident in her office, it appeared to have a disarming effect on my colleagues and from then on my relationship with all the staff was always very friendly and cordial.

Another incident occurred that again brought home to me the great divide between the two communities. It happened when I was being driven back to the hospital by a Roman Catholic priest. He stopped his car to let me out some distance from the hospital and informed me that it would not be a good thing for me to be seen being dropped off outside the hospital by him. Oddly enough, I never seemed to cross the 'great divide' very much, for I used to spend my off-duty time with my aunt, on my mother's side, and her family, who were Protestants and lived a short distance from Belfast.

My work in the hospital was very interesting and satisfying. There were two Resident Surgical Officers, another doctor and myself, on the staff. We did alternate periods of twenty-four hours on duty dealing with all the emergency admissions. We were the senior members of the resident staff, which were twenty-eight in number, and included a Resident Penicillin Officer, Pathologist, Anaesthetist, Radiographer, Dispenser, etc.

I got on well with the consultants. I learned a great deal from spending my off-duty time in their operating theatres, and wards, and attending their out-patients clinics, which, in the years ahead, helped me in advancing my career in surgery. One particular surgeon, who subsequently became a long-standing friend of mine, had a reputation for being a very 'fast operator'. He was a surgeon of some renown and had served with great distinction during the War. On this return from the War, the first operation he performed was an appendectomy. I well remember the gathering of doctors in the operating theatre, all intent on estimating the length of time the surgeon took to do the operation, and seeing if he would break his pre-war record, which I believe he did. I should mention that the patient made a good recovery from his operation.

My work, occasionally, entailed the giving of anaesthetics. I remember giving an anaesthetic for a neurosurgeon. He had inherited an orthopaedic ward from a surgeon who had retired and was left some cases waiting to have minor operations. One of these cases was having a foot operation, which usually entailed the application of a tourniquet to the patient's leg, in order to reduce the blood loss during the operation. However, the neurosurgeon intimated to me that, since in a head operation he would reduce blood loss by tilting the patient with his head up and almost in a vertical position, we should use the reverse position for a foot operation. The end result was he did the operating standing on a stool, whilst I gave the anaesthetic kneeling on the floor!

I used to spend a day, from time to time, doing hernia operations in a small hospital in the country, away from the hurly-burly of my busy own hospital. Apart from working in a peaceful and tranquil environment, the anaesthetist and I had the added bonus of enjoying a very nice lunch, but, however, in return for what we enjoyed, we had to bring our patients down a flight of stairs on a stretcher to the operating theatre, and back up again after their operations.

Toward the end of my sojourn in Belfast, doctors were returning home from the War and were taking up appointments in the hospital. One of them, a very fine young doctor, joined our resident staff as a house physician. He appeared to be somewhat depressed, uncommunicative and withdrawn, but nevertheless always pleasant and co-operative. He never talked about his wartime experiences. However, I eventually got to know that he was in Singapore at the time of its capture by the Japanese and had performed an act of great bravery and gallantry when they overran the Military Hospital and massacred some of the patients and staff. As I understood it, he was in the operating theatre when the Japanese entered it, and because of his presence of mind and ingenuity, he managed to save the lives of some members of the theatre staff by hiding them in a linen cupboard. For his heroic action he was awarded the MC, and I am pleased to say that some years later he reached the zenith of his field in our profession.

I left Belfast in February 1946, not knowing that I would return there thirty years later, in the capacity of Director of Army Surgery. After returning to Dublin, I took a year's sabbath, undertaking a postgraduate course in surgery, in preparation for my Final Fellowship of the Royal College of Surgeons in Ireland examination, which I passed in March 1947.

During my preparation for the examination, it was wont, that I rekindled my interest in Surgical Anatomy. In doing so, I came to know a Demonstrator in Anatomy, who was a brilliant anatomist, and at the same time a well-known and beloved character in the Medical Schools of Dublin. He was completely dedicated to the study of Anatomy. He had a propensity for producing a bone from his pocket, at any time when he came in contact with students outside the Anatomy Department. The contact was often made in a pub frequented by students. On one occasion, in the pub, he produced a large animal bone from a parcel he had been carrying, saying that he had found the bone on a pavement when he stepped off a bus. He then proceeded to question the students on its identity, and subsequently to demonstrate its anatomical features to them.

Chapter 5

A Glorious Three Years in Lancashire

In March 1947, I assumed the role of Resident Surgical Officer in a busy hospital in Lancashire. I enjoyed my sojourn in Lancashire very much. The more I got to know the Lancastrians, the more I came to admire and respect them for their kindness, friendliness and straightforward attitude to their fellow human beings. I had a high regard for the nursing, medical and administrative staff of the hospital for their integrity, and ability.

As time went on, I became competent in being able to deal with the various aspects of emergency surgery my work entailed. I also developed experience in the many fields of cold surgery, including the orthopaedic, gynaecological and ENT fields, by my involvement in the visiting surgeons' routine operating theatre lists.

The most memorable case I had to deal with was a pregnancy that had developed away from the womb in the abdominal cavity and had ruptured. At that time, only a small number of such cases had been reported in the literature.

Another unusual case, a case of a young boy suffering from acute Pyloric Obstruction, i.e., obstruction to the outlet of the stomach, again illustrated the fact that one had always to be prepared to come across the unexpected finding at an operation. At operation, I found that this patient's obstruction was caused by the impaction of a large bolus of chewed up newspaper in the stomach outlet! It turned out that the boy was an habitual chewer of newspapers.

In the absence of the modern high-powered means of investigation, e.g., scanning techniques, the use of good powers of observation and deduction in those days was mandatory when a diagnosis was being considered. That point of view is exemplified in the case that was presented to me by the Visiting Physician on duty one Saturday morning. An

21

elderly man alleged to be suffering from a stroke had been admitted to his ward. The physician found that he had a small bruise on his temple. The patient lived alone and was found unconscious on his kitchen floor, near a stove. Radiological examination, incidentally, did not reveal any evidence of fracture of the skull. The problem that confronted us was simply: did he suffer from a stroke, and as a result became unconscious and fall to the ground, and sustain the bruise on his head, or did he accidentally fall, and sustain a head injury *per se*? I agreed to carry out an exploratory operation, i.e., a craniotomy at the site of the bruise, on the grounds that, if he was suffering from a stroke, there was nothing specific that could be done to affect the course of the illness, but however, if he was suffering from a head injury *per se*, an operation could resolve its effects. At the operation, I did in fact find out that he had an Extra-Dural haemorhage, resulting from his injury and which had caused a blood clot to press on his brain. I am pleased to record that he made a good recovery from his operation.

I had many traumatic experiences associated with my work. The one I shall always remember occurred at the time one of our visiting surgeons resigned rather hurriedly in order that he could take up a Professorial appointment overseas. He left me with a backlog of cases to deal with, pending the appointment of his successor. The cases included a number of circumcisions and tonsillectomies, on children, which were carried out on a Sunday morning on the kitchen table in the patients' home, with a GP giving the anaesthetic and the District Nurse assisting at the operation. After completion of the first case, which was a guillotine tonsillectomy, the patient stopped breathing. However, mercifully, after a few moments he commenced breathing again and subsequently made a full recovery from the operation. I was so horrified by what happened, I immediately abandoned doing any further surgery on kitchen tables.

I recall my first experience of attending a coroner's inquest, mainly because of a somewhat hilarious cameo that presented during it. An elderly lady died during an operation to discover the cause of her jaundice. At the operation, I found that she had an irremovable cancer of her pancreas with widespread dissemination of the tumour in the liver. At the subsequent inquest, when giving evidence, I had got to the stage of being about to report my findings at the operation, when the Coroner, who wore a pince-nez on the tip of his nose, and was seated on a high dais, interrupted me and looking down at me, enquired if there were any gall stones found at the operation. When I replied there weren't any, he turned to the jury in amazement and exclaimed, 'Remember ladies and gentlemen, no gall stones.' Until then, I had felt I was giving evidence at what was supposed to be a routine and straightforward inquest! Because at this stage, I hadn't yet reported my findings at the operation, the jury looked perplexed by my failure to find any gall stones. I then realised that gall stones, apart from being a common cause of jaundice, were in the laymans mind, a common cause of death. Needless to say, when I finished reading my report on the findings at the operation, 'normal service' as we say nowadays, was resumed at the inquest.

I went to race meetings on two occasions. The first occasion, the Grand National meeting at Liverpool, was a financial disaster for me. Some of the hospital staff, fortunately not many, gave me money to put on Sheila's Cottage in the National for them. My father came over from Ireland for the race. In order to give him a good view of the race, we spent some time in moving from one grandstand to another, with the result that when we did find a good position to look down on the course from, the race was about to get underway and it was too late for me to place my bets! Sheila's Cottage won the race. His price was twenty-seven to one, which meant that I had to pay my colleagues a large sum of money from my own pocket. Fortunately, the other occasion when I went to a race meeting had a happy ending. I remember the occasion very well. It was the New Year's Day meeting at Manchester. The pathologist and I were invited into the owners' and trainers' enclosure. To cut a long story short, by the time we came to the last race, an air of gloom and doom had descended on the small group of owners and trainers who were our hosts. They hadn't backed a winner all day! My fancy for the race was a thirty-three to one outsider. At first they laughed at my choice, but, however, soon afterwards something made them change their minds and they backed my horse. I can still remember my horse at the end of the race coming out of the mist and winning by a distance! Our hosts, needless to say, were overjoyed. They had recouped their losses. One of them subsequently insisted on taking my colleague and me for a meal on our journey back to the hospital.

During my time in Lancashire, I decided it was time I obtained my driving licence. After having some driving lessons, I duly presented myself for a driving test. However, the examiner failed to keep the appointment with me. Soon afterwards, I was issued with another appointment for my test. This time the examiner was ready and waiting to commence the test. He appeared to be very bad-tempered. He gave me no apology for not keeping the previous appointment. During the test he gave me tasks to perform which were impossible to carry out. One concerned entering a main road at a 'T' junction. The approach road was on a steep hill! I was to enter the main road using only hand signals. Another impossible task, was to perform a three-point turn in a road that was not much wider than the length of the car! At the end of the test, he informed me that by right he should fail me, but however the consequences of my letter of complaint were such that, he had no option but to pass me. I assured him that I had not written any letter of complaint. It subsequently, transpired that, my Hospital Superintendent had written the letter.

The hospital was run efficiently by a fairly elderly Superintendent and a small staff of clerks and typists. However, the Superintendent always kept a tight rein on the hospital's finances. It was my duty to report on the surgical work done at the monthly meetings of the Medical Advisory Committee, of which the Superintendent was Chairman. On one occasion, I reported on the much greater use of 'high' spinal anaesthesia by the surgeons. Spinal anaesthesia could only be used for operations on the lower limbs and the trunk as far up as the upper abdomen. The Superintendent, having misunderstood what I had said, and thinking we now had advanced the field of spinal anaesthesia to include 'eye operations', immediately congratulated us on the financial savings we were making by not having to use the more expensive inhalational gas anaesthesia.

Alas, from our dearly beloved Superintendent's point of view, the NHS was established in 1948 and our voluntary hospital became absorbed into it, losing its autonomy and becoming amalgamated administratively with another hospital. A Hospital Management Committee was set up to run both hospitals jointly. The Superintendent and his staff were replaced by a Secretary with a large staff, which included finance, personnel and supply officers. At that time, many of us hospital doctors were amazed and critical of what was happening to the running of our hospital. However, as time went on, we became conditioned to the new order of things. In spite of all the advantages the NHS had to offer to the hospitals, I could foresee that the hospitals would lose out on the very valuable work done by the visiting surgeons any time of day or night on a voluntary basis, now that the specialists working in the NHS were contracted to work on a fixed-time sessional basis.

I used to fly home to Dublin on my weekends off duty. Two incidents occurred during these journeys. One was embarrassing, and the other, terrifying, to say the least.

On one occasion, because, I suspect, I was such a regular traveller, and always had very little luggage, I was very thoroughly interrogated, and indeed strip-searched by the immigration officers at Liverpool airport. On the other occasion, we were making our approach to Liverpool airport in visibility that was so poor that one could hardly see the airport buildings in the distance. In spite of the very poor visibility, our pilot attempted to land our plane. His attempt at landing failed, and as we regained height, we narrowly missed colliding with some buildings in the vicinity of the airport. Indeed, I still can remember seeing the roofs and chimney-pots of the buildings only a few feet below us. We subsequently landed at Manchester airport. There we were taken to a room away from the main concourse of the terminal building, where we were given liquid refreshment, and allowed some time to recover from our ordeal, before proceeding to Liverpool by road. I can still recall, as I sat in that room, observing the severe degree of emotional shock, most of the passengers were suffering from. An air hostess, who was very calm and collected when caring for her passengers on the plane immediately after the incident, however, did not now help matters, by repeating over and over again in her conversation with the passengers, that the pilot should never have attempted to land the plane in such dense fog.

One morning in January 1950, I received a visit from a man from the 'Ministry'. He was dressed in a dark suit, wore a bowler hat and carried an umbrella and a brief case. He intimated to me that he had something of great personal importance to discuss with me. Having sat him down at a table in my bedroom, he opened his brief case and produced some documents. Reading from the documents, he gave me an account of all my movements in and out of England since I first arrived in the country in August 1943. He then stated that I had gone beyond the time allowed to an Irish citizen to work in England before he becomes eligible for National Service. He informed me that there were two options open to me. One was to leave the country immediately, and not return in the forseeable future, if I wished to avoid doing National Service. The other was, of course, to agree to being called up immediately for my National Service, since I would soon have passed the 30 years call-up age limit. I agreed to be called up. However, subsequently, because I felt that my prospects of establishing a worthwhile career in surgery in my present hospital were bright, I decided to appeal against my call-up. The hospital supported my appeal and, in due course, I presented myself to the Secretary of War Central Medical Committee in London. My appeal, however, was rejected, but I did succeed in making the point that, in my opinion, the Committee was mostly made up of doctors from London and was not sufficiently representative of doctors working in peripheral areas such as mine in the North of England. I also found out whilst I was in London, that the main reason for my urgent call-up concerned the fact that a national tabloid newspaper had given great publicity to an allegation of a shortage of surgeons in Malaya, where the Army was engaged in an anti-terrorist campaign.

Chapter 6

National Service

Having passed my Entry medical examination, I reported for duty at Ash Vale, near Aldershot. After three weeks of basic training, I was told to report to the Administration Officer, who informed me that I had been posted to Aquaba, which was in the Persian Gulf, as an RMO. I informed the officer that I was a surgeon and expected to undertake duties in keeping with my specialist status. He ignored my protestations and handed me my posting order, which instructed me to proceed on two weeks embarkation leave. I had only just arrived on leave in Dublin when I received a telephone call from him, requesting me to return to England as soon as possible as there was an error in my posting, which he was not responsible for. My posting should have been to Malaya as a surgeon. I refused to return until after I had completed my two weeks' leave in Ireland. He acquiesced and agreed to me completing my leave. He arranged for me to have my necessary inoculations in an Army Medical Centre in Northern Ireland.

I departed from Dublin in June 1950. Apart from spending periods of leave there, I was never to reside in Ireland again. Soon after I returned to England I flew to Singapore in a BOAC Super De Lux Constellation aircraft, as a first-class passenger. We had a five-hour stopover in Rome, with lunch and a guided tour of the city, an overnight stop in Cairo, where we stayed in a luxurious hotel, and breakfast in Karachi. It was in the latter city that I gained at firsthand an insight into one of the perils of living or travelling in the East. At breakfast, a fellow traveller stopped me from drinking a glass of water and then drew my attention to a report in a local newspaper of a large outbreak of Cholera in the suburb of the city we were in.

At Karachi, I said goodbye to my erstwhile fellow traveller. He was a deep-sea diver employed by the Royal Navy. He was about to undertake

Departure from Dublin.

Rome, – Appian Way.

his last diving mission before retiring. During the flight he had drunk a lot of alcohol, and had become very morose. During his career as a deep-sea diver, he had experienced many mishaps, some of which could have had dire consequences. He was very fatalistic, and was convinced that something dreadful would happen to him during his last undertaking. Nothing I said seemed to compose him. In the end I turned to the subject of religion. However he confessed he was an atheist. I then asked him what went through his mind when he felt he was near to dying in the worst of his mishaps. He recalled that he had said to himself, 'O my God I am going to die.' My response to what he had said was to inform him that he had just given me sufficient evidence for me to feel he was not an atheist, and had a belief in God. Just then, we were about to land at Karachi. We fastened our seat belts. Nothing more was said. I hoped that the final part of our discussion might strike a chord that would eventually bring peace and tranquillity to his troubled mind.

I arrived in Singapore on a Saturday morning, three days after we left London. When I left the air-conditioned cabin of our aircraft, I emerged into an almost unbearable hot and humid atmosphere. My arrival in Singapore appeared to be unexpected. There was no one there to meet me. After a while, an Army officer, who became aware of my plight, kindly gave me a lift in his jeep to the RAMC Officers' Mess. Over the weekend I was well looked after by the officers living in the Mess, I am pleased to say.

On Monday morning, I was taken to the Military Hospital, and introduced to the Administrative Officer. The latter officer immediately, after I had entered his office, began to admonish me for not saluting him. I felt that his attitude to me was understandable, when I remembered that I was only a very junior National Service Captain and he was a very senior Regular Army Major! Soon after my 'dressing down', the CO appeared and beckoned me into his office. As a fellow graduate of my university, he welcomed me to Singapore.

Before taking up my surgical duties in Malaya, I was detailed to do two weeks relief duties for the senior surgeon in the Singapore hospital. During the time I spent in the latter hospital, through my own fault entirely, I did not make many friends. Having just left a very busy civilian hospital, where I was enjoying my work very much, and had many friends, I felt somewhat depressed and unable to adjust to my new and strange environment. However, I hasten to add, my fellow medical officers did all they could to make my short sojourn in Singapore as pleasurable as possible.

I was subsequently posted to the Kamunting Military Hospital in Taiping, which is in the north of Malaya. I travelled there overnight by train. The terrorist campaign was, at that time, at its height. During our journey, our train was derailed by a land-mine. Fortunately, nobody on the train was seriously injured, most of the bomb blast being taken up by a dummy engine in front of the train. After some hours we were rescued and taken by a relief train to our destination, which we reached at about four o'clock in the morning. Having had a few hours sleep, I reported to the Commanding Officer of the hospital who, after a few words of greeting, demanded that I get my hair cut. After just completing a very long and hazardous jour-ney from Singapore, I was not in the mood at that par-

Entrance and Surgical Ward – British Military Hospital, Kamunting.

Taiping.

ticular time to even consider having my hair cut. His reaction to my refusal to was call his chief clerk into his office and request him to fetch the barber. My response to his action was, to wish him a good morning, give him a smart salute, and march out of his office. Subsequently, regrettably for a while, our relationship both on and off duty was never very cordial, to say the least.

Soon after I commenced my duties in the hospital, I examined the wife of a young officer. She was in the early stages of pregnancy, and was suffering from some form of mental stress resulting from it. We had an airstrip not far from the hospital which we used for the aero-medical evacuation of casualties to Singapore. I had her flown down to Singapore to be seen by a psychiatrist there. Sometime later, when she was travelling back from Singapore by air, she developed a severe haemorrhage. When she was admitted to hospital, she was very ill from loss of blood from her womb. Whilst she was in Singapore, she had a termination of her pregnancy, which had been advised by the psychiatrists who had been treating her. In spite of resuscitation with a large volume of blood, she continued to bleed, and it soon became apparent that surgical intervention was necessary to stop her haemorrhaging. I received written consent from the patient and her husband to perform the operation and carry out any procedure that was necessary. At the operation, I found that she had a bifid womb and both ovaries riddled with tumour tissue. I felt that the best thing to do was to remove her womb and her ovaries, which I did. She made a good recovery from her operation. Subsequently she was referred to a gynaecologist in Singapore for any follow-up treatment of her ovarian tumour that might be necessary. However, on the day after the operation, an aftermath to it occurred which affected me personally. The CO was unaware that I had obtained written consent, not only for performing an operation on the patient, but also, for performing any operative procedure that I deemed was necessary. This presumably was, because, the relevant documents being so important medico-legally, I had safeguarded them. He arranged for me to be interviewed in his office by a Senior Medical Officer from Army Headquarters, as a consequence of his feeling, that I could be considered to be somewhat professionally negligent. However, after I produced the written consent forms, the Senior Officer apologised to me for my professional integrity having in any way been questioned. The matter was then closed, and the latter officer and I proceeded to admire the lovely tropical plants that were growing outside the CO's office! After this incident, the CO and I settled our differences, and became good friends.

The staff of the hospital consisted of the Commanding Officer, Matron and her staff of QA nursing officers, an Administrative Officer, Quartermaster, Surgeon, Physician, Anaesthetist, General Duty Medical Officer, Dental Officer, Other Rank male Nursing Orderlies, Laboratory Technicians, Radiographers and a Company Officer and RSM and their staff. There were 100 beds in the hospital. The wards were wooden rectangular one-story buildings, sited in parallel rows on either side of a long open corridor. They were not air-conditioned, but instead had ceiling fans. In the operating theatre, cooling fans were used in lieu of air-conditioning. I refurbished a small storeroom near the operating theatre and equipped it with enough cooling fans to make it suitable for the care of seriously ill patients with high temperatures. We received casualties at the rate of about two to three a day, several days each week, with peak intakes of about ten or twelve in a day every few weeks. Their injuries were caused mainly by small arms weapons e.g., SLRs and machine-guns. The strategy used in the war against the terrorists was, incidentally, aimed at preventing them from getting supplies and succour from villagers and also from intimidating them. In addition, the strategy aimed at seeking out terrorist camps in the jungle and ambushing the terrorists as they entered them or left them. On the other hand, the enemy sought to ambush our troops as they made their way through the jungle. Our soldiers also undertook the duties of assisting the police in protecting the rubber planters and their plantations from terrorist actions.

I also helped to provide medical care for the local indigenous people by acting as surgeon to the local civilian hospital.

Amongst the Army casualties we treated, there were many who had committed acts of bravery and heroism, which were unheralded and received no publicity. I recall one such case very well. A corporal, in charge of the guard at his unit, was sitting in the guardroom writing a letter to his wife, when a terrorist entered and stabbed him. Although seriously injured, he still managed to alert the guard by firing off a round from his weapon. The terrorist immediately fled without accomplishing his mission of stealing weapons and ammunition from the guardroom. I subsequently operated on him and removed his damaged spleen. I am pleased to say that he made a good recovery from his injury.

Recalling the above case of the serviceman having to have his spleen removed as a result of terrorist action, reminds me of a similar case, but with regrettably a different outcome. A local civilian, a Malayan, was stabbed by a terrorist and subsequently admitted to the civilian hospital. I operated on him and removed his spleen. Unfortunately, about a week after the operation, his condition rapidly deteriorated and he died. At the subsequent coroner's inquest, a medico-legal problem presented. His post-mortem examination had revealed that the cause of his death was fulminating Malaria. The Coroner was intent on bringing in a verdict, as a result of the latter findings, of death from natural causes. However, I argued that it was well-known clinically that loss of one's spleen could lower a patient's resistant to Malaria, and that therefore his death was precipitated by the injury inflicted on him by the terrorist.

One of my most interesting experiences began on a Sunday afternoon, when I was awoken from my post-prandial nap by a mess waiter, who informed me that a local civilian was anxiously waiting to speak to a doctor. When I spoke to him, he informed me that his wife was having a baby, and was in some distress, in some small kampong (village) in the ulu (jungle) not far from the hospital. Without thinking I followed him into the jungle and, needless to say, this was a silly thing to do, as I might easily have been walking into a trap set by the terrorists. However, when I reached my destination, I found a young lady in the throes of the final stage of childbirth. I assisted her with the completion of what turned out, in the end, to be a normal delivery of her baby and subsequently tied off her cord temporarily with my shoelace. I then returned to the hospital and arranged for her to be brought into hospital for after-care of her childbirth.

My post-prandial naps could be quite eventful. On one occasion, I woke up to see a very large spider making its way towards me across the floor. I succeeded in getting it into a box and presented it to a pathologist for identification. He subsequently informed me that it was one of the most dangerous spiders in Malaya, and that its bite could be lethal. On another occasion, I developed an excruciating toothache after lunch. Previously, when I was working in the hospital in Lancashire, I suffered from toothache for some time. One of our visiting surgeons very kindly drove me to a hospital where a colleague worked in a high-powered Maxillofacial unit. The latter specialist agreed to extract the offending tooth at the end of his operating theatre list. However, before he undertook the procedure, he warned me that he had not done a dental extraction for about twenty years! He also informed me that his anaesthetist had gone to lunch and, if I had no objection, a young houseman would give me the anaesthetic. The upshot of all this was that I woke up from the anaesthetic just as the surgeon was attempting to extract the tooth! I remember that moment well. I was sitting up on the operating table, holding on to the arm of the theatre sister and resisting the attempts of the young houseman to hold me down. The culmination of the surgeon's efforts was a fracture of the tooth, and as a result the roots of the tooth were left *in situ*. Fortunately, I had not had a recurrence of the toothache until now in Malaya. This time our dental surgeon, seeing I was in agony, gave me a large whiskey and took me over to his surgery, where he proceeded to extract the roots under local anaesthetic, and I hasten to add painlessly and successfully!

I had one narrow escape from being ambushed by the terrorists. There was a rest-house on top of a hill not far from the hospital, where one could spend a short time away from the heat and humidity, because of its high altitude. On my way up to the rest-house one day, the vehicle some distance ahead of mine was ambushed, but fortunately there were no serious casualties.

At the back of our hospital there was a Field Ambulance. It was located not far from our operating theatre. Its CO was a district disciplinarian, and Monday morning was the time he seemed to dish out most of the week's punishments. His RSM was not immune to the lashings of his tongue. My operating theatre technicians used to watch out for the reappearance of the RSM from the CO's office and could tell when he had received a dressing down from the CO, by the way he would pass on his telling off to the first soldier he encountered. He apparently was never at a loss in finding some fault in any soldier's demeanour or dress.

There was a club in the local town used mainly by the planters as a haven from the stresses of the terrorists' campaign. It was also used by Army officers for meals and parties at weekends. I attended a St Patrick's Night party there. During the party, a lady came to talk to me about her amah, who was ill. She wanted to know what might be the cause of her illness. At that time I had been very busy, and as a result I was enjoying my few hours of relaxation in the club. I felt that this was not the time or place to be discussing a patient's illness, and told the good lady so very politely, I believe. The next morning, I was summoned to the office of a senior officer at HQ. The officer informed me that I had been accused of insulting a lady at the party on the previous night. When I related the circumstances of the incident and what I had actually said to the lady, he laughed and apologised for the inconveniences he had caused me by summoning me to his office.

Convoy of vehicles being escorted by security forces.

In recalling my tour of duty in North Malaya, I shall always remember the dedication of an RC priest to his flock. In his travels around the country caring for members of his church, he ignored the security regulation of always being accompanied by an escort of the security forces. In his endeavours to cover as much ground as widely and quickly as possible, he travelled alone in a jeep driven by a Malayan soldier who was very familiar with the area he had to cover in his parish so to speak. He would be gone for days, and one wondered if he would be killed by the terrorists and never be seen again. He became somewhat of a legend. On one occasion he caught up with a column of vehicles belonging to a Guards Regiment on a dangerous road in the jungle. He persuaded his driver to drive past them, and then, having got ahead of them, he stopped his vehicle, bringing the column of vehicles to a halt. A very irate CO demanded to know what the hell did he think he was doing and why he was travelling alone unescorted. His reply was that he wanted to hear the confessions of the Catholics in the CO's Regiment. He, then, without further ado, proceeded to walk back along the column of vehicles indicating he was available for hearing of confessions. On another occasion he was travelling on a road through the jungle, when his driver suddenly stopped the vehicle, got out, and disappeared into the jungle. For a few minutes he lived in the fear of being ambushed by the terrorists. However, his driver soon reappeared, and apologised for leaving him and told him he had to stop and spend a penny!

A range of hills could be seen in the distance from the rear of the hospital, and it used to be said by the oldest inhabitants of the Mess that, as time went on, the hills would seem to be getting closer to you and that was the time when you would like a change of scenery. The latter time for me was slowly approaching in the autumn of 1950 when the CO asked to see me urgently. When I entered his office, he was speaking on the telephone to our Senior Medical Officer Colonel Alexander Drummond at Army Headquarters in Kuala Lumpur. The latter officer had only recently arrived out from the UK and, in taking over his new appointment, was in the process of reorganising the staffing of the Military Hospitals under his Command. In his conversation on the telephone with our CO he was informing him, that I was to be posted to the Base Hospital i.e., the Kinrara Military Hospital, Kuala Lumpur. My posting was to take place very soon. At that time, as I was looking after about twelve patients with serious gunshot wounds, I did not wish to hand over the management of some of these cases to another surgeon whilst they were still recovering from their wounds. Consequently, I resolutely refused to accept the posting order. When the CO informed him of my refusal to accept the order, he instructed the CO to advise me that my refusal could involve me in court martial proceedings. However, I still refused to comply with his order, whereupon he informed the CO that he would fly up to Taiping on the following morning to see me. When he arrived at my hospital, I immediately took him to see my patients. Having been a surgeon himself, he became very interested in the discussion I was having with him about their management and progress. He was very kind, and understanding of my point of view concerning the timing of the handover of my cases to another surgeon. He acquiesced and delayed my posting for a few days. We subsequently became very good friends, and some years later I was to become indebted to him for the guidance and encouragement he gave me concerning my career in surgery.

Kinrara Military Hospital was much larger and busier, but its layout was similar to my previous hospital. It had more specialists on its staff and had its own airstrip and, because of the use of helicopters for the evacuations of casualties, it had a very wide encachment area. Many of the casualties we received were Gurkha servicemen, for whom I had a high regard and admiration, not only their bravery, but also for the stoicism and cheerfulness, in spite of the very serious injuries they sometimes sustained.

Soon after I arrived in Kinrara, a new operating theatre sister was due to commence duty in the hospital. Her name was Capt. Eileen White, and she came from County Cork. She arrived in the theatre at 7.30 a.m. one morning, just as I was about to commence a long list of operations on G.S.W. cases. She had been expected to arrive the previous evening but, however, the convoy she was travelling in on her way down from the Cameron Highlands, was ambushed by terrorists, and as a result, she spent some time on the roadside tending to the wounded. I remember when she walked into the theatre, looking aghast at her dishevelled uniform and her blackened face, I asked her who she was and what she was doing in my operating theatre. In reply, she asked me who I was!

In October 1950, I was promoted to the rank of Major.

The CO of the hospital was a highly efficient officer. He had only recently arrived from London, and had been selected by our Senior Medical Officer for the appointment. Most of the hospital medical officers were, like myself, National Service officers. They were highly skilled professionals and dedicated in their care of their patients. However, they were looking forward to the day when they would be returned to civilian life. To help them come to terms with their temporary sojourn in the Army, they displayed a keen sense of humour which, I recall on one occasion, was misdirected. A medical officer, when answering the telephone in the mess one day, exclaimed, 'This is Battersea Power Station.' The senior officer making the call from HQ replied, without thinking, 'Sorry, wrong number', and apologised for any inconvenience he had caused. The officer at HQ soon came to his senses and, in due course, the medical officer found himself doing duty with a Field Ambulance in the jungle. On another occasion, an officer in answering the telephone, announced his name, rank, serial number and date of demobilization and then asked the caller what was his.

The medical officers were not particularly enamoured with the CO's dedication to seeing that they discharged their non-medical duties efficiently. They evolved a plan of action to exclude him from their conversations in the mess. Their scheme was simple. All conversations, not involving clinical matters, were to revolve around imagining the hospital was a railway station! Each MO had a part to play in the running of the station. I was appointed stationmaster. The hospital wards were the station platforms. For sometime the CO couldn't understand what, to say the least, was going on and naturally became very worried. One day he took me to one side and confided in me that he would very much like to become part of the railway station set up. After a meeting with my colleagues, it was agreed that he could take over my appointment as stationmaster and I would become a ticket collector. As a result, relations with our CO became very cordial and, to coin a phrase, we all lived happily ever after. Soon interest was lost in the railway station and our conversations reverted back to reality. Before that happened, some mail was delivered with the address of 'Kinrara Railway Station' on it. However, I must hastily add that recourse to the aforementioned fantasy was not the result of any lowering of the morale of the MOs, indeed their moral was always high.

The time I spent working in the Military Hospital was the busiest period of my whole career in surgery. It was not unusual for me, in dealing with an influx of casualties suffering from gunshot wounds, to have to spend most of the day and night operating on them.

The Senior Medical Officer at Headquarters spent a good deal of his time visiting the hospital and could be seen in it at any time of day or night. On one Sunday afternoon, as I was in the process of resuscitating a large number of casualties, he appeared on the scene. Seeing how busy I was, he gave assistance with putting up 'drips'. Later, when I was about to operate on the first case, he volunteered to assist me. This did not please my operating theatre staff, perhaps for the reason that they did not like the idea of having their work being scrutinised by such a senior officer. The anaesthetist got to know about their feelings and, as if by accident, touched his sterile gown. This meant that the officer had to leave the table and change gown and gloves. He did not return to the table, however, because he could see that my theatre sister was coping quite adequately with assisting me.

My most interesting experience whilst serving in Malaya, concerned my visit to a leper colony. I was asked to perform a prostatectomy operation on a very elderly Chinese resident in the colony. He had been in the colony since before the last World War and became the first patient to be treated in the colony successfully, when the drug Sulphone came into use towards the end of the War. He was the hospital staff's prize ex-patient and they didn't want anything to happen to him. I am pleased to say that he recovered well from the operation. The colony was run by an English doctor, who was the superintendent of the hospital. His wife was the matron. The colony was more or less self-sufficient. It produced its own food supply and ran its own services i.e., police, fire brigade, judicial, etc. There were many small communities within the colony, farming, carpentry, etc. Once their disease had become controlled, the patients were discharged from hospital to a community for rehabilitation, with occupational therapy. During the War, when the Japanese overran Malaya, they avoided entering the colony for fear of catching the disease and the colony became completely isolated from the outside world.

Towards the end of my sojourn in Malaya, two events occurred, one of which was to effect my life on a long-term basis, the other on a very short-term basis: the former event, a very happy one, my engagement to my operating theatre sister, Eileen White, and the latter, a matter of tasting one's own medicine, an illness. My illness could be described as a fever of unknown origin, so unknown that my colleagues looking after me cast a very wide net in their search for its aetiology. I had several forms of different drug therapy, through no fault of theirs. However, as time went on I began to feel well again, although at the same time, my fever persisted but happily at a low grade. At that time, I realised that my two years of National Service were coming to an end. To make sure that I would be on the next troopship leaving Singapore, I decided to get myself out of the clutches of my colleagues, the physicians, and take my discharge from the hospital. I was allowed to go to our convalescent hospital in the Cameron Highlands and stay there whilst I was waiting to embark on the troopship. Subsequently my fever completely subsided during the voyage home.

Capt. Eileen White – My operating theatre sister.

Before closing this saga on my illness, I feel I must relate an amusing episode that occurred soon after I was admitted to hospital. A very great friend of mine, who was a Medical Officer in North Malaya, came to visit me. He decided to stay in the hospital for a few days and, in order to do so, he got himself admitted to the hospital on the pretext that he was suffering from diarrhoea! Much to his disappointment, he was discharged after 48 hours on the grounds that he had been unable to produce the necessary specimen for examination before any treatment could be commenced!

Chapter 7

Return to Civilian Life

Eileen and I returned to the UK on the *Empire Trooper*. The ship was very crowded with troops returning from the war in Korea. I shared a small cabin with three other officers. We had to take it in turns to dress and wash ourselves. However, I saw very little of my fellow officers, as they seemed to spend all their time, day and night, playing bridge. Our journey to Southampton took about six weeks. As acting surgeon on board the ship, I was only called upon once to see a patient. He was suffering from acute appendicitis. We disembarked him at Port Said. We also stopped at Colombo, Aden, Malta and Gibraltar. Our voyage was uneventful, apart from a breakdown in the ship's air cooling system, which resulted in the

Empire Trooper.

42

Aden.

ship having to steam backwards going through the Red Sea, to allow the
ventilating shafts to suck air into the system.

After completion of our disembarkation leave we were both demobbed.
We subsequently got married in June 1952. We spent our honeymoon on
the south coast and a good deal of that time was spent applying for a
hospital surgical appointment. To begin with, whilst waiting for a suitable
long-term appointment, I applied for a short-term appointment as a Senior
Registrar in a West of England teaching hospital. The hospital found us a
very nice flat to live in. The hospital staff were very friendly and kind.
After the mental and physical stress and strains of my army service in
Malaya, I found peace and tranquillity working in this civilian hospital.
My memories of my work there include a male patient aged about ninety,
who, when recovering from an appendicectomy operation, agitated to be
discharged in order that he could return to work cycling around his village

Suez Canal.

as a postman. I remember an embarrassing situation that arose in the operating theatre one day. My consultant decided to give a talk to the students on the operation I was performing. After he left the theatre, I found, to my horror, an error in my surgical technique which had occurred as a result of me being enraptured by the words of wisdom being uttered by the consultant. To my great embarrassment, I had to redo part of the operative procedure, which was partial removal of the stomach, in front of the students who had remained to watch the completion of the operation.

One of my colleagues, on another firm, was very subservient to his consultant and was always at his beck and call. One day, I overheard his houseman as he followed him round the hospital, hum the famous aria from La Boheme, using his own words, 'Your tiny pile is frozen. Let me warm it into life', as a symbol of my colleague's deference to his consultant.

Finally, I recall operating on a patient my consultant sent into the hospital one night. I operated on the case, a semi-emergency case, not knowing that he was a private patient, the consultant was going to operate on early the following morning. Fortunately, the patient recovered well from his operation but, until he did so, I had a very worrying time. However, my consultant, from the very beginning of the affair, was most understanding and forgiving.

I left the hospital in October 1952, having had a very pleasant re-entry to civilian surgical practice. I am pleased to say Eileen enjoyed our short stay in the West of England.

Some twenty years later, I was delighted to be remembered by the staff of the hospital, when they invited me to attend a function that was being held in honour of one of the consultants who was retiring, and who was one of the surgeons I worked under.

I was subsequently employed as Senior Registrar in a hospital in an eastern suburb of London. It was quite a busy hospital. I worked under two consultants, one of whom was employed full-time, and the other, who was on the staff of a London teaching hospital, part-time. They were both very kind to me and I got on well with them. They delegated the entire responsibility of the running of the Surgical Unit to me during their absence on holidays, etc.

I enjoyed my work very much, in spite of having to spend long hours in the hospital. The members of the Surgical Unit worked as a team in close harmony with each other, and in a very happy atmosphere. I enhanced my surgical experience a great deal. In particular, I learned a lot more about bone and joint surgery, as a result of taking my difficult problem cases to the London teaching hospital clinic of a very renowned orthopaedic surgeon. Eileen worked in a private nursing home and she enjoyed her return to nursing duties very much. We lived in a comfortable flat in a quiet residential area. Our social life evolved from getting to know doctors and their wives introduced to us by my brother, who was a GP in an adjacent London borough. In every way, between work and play, we lived a full but peaceful and contented life.

However, my goal in the long term was to find a suitable consultants appointment. Regrettably, consultants posts were in short supply. After three unsuccessful applications for such posts, I became somewhat optimistic about my fourth attempt. I found there was a vacancy in a

North London hospital, where a friend of mine, who served with me as a physician in Malaya, was on its staff. He assured me that, as a result of the work he had done canvassing on my behalf, I had a good chance of being successful in getting the appointment. There were four of us short-listed for the appointment. Little did we know, the most junior of the four of us had already been earmarked for the appointment. I presumed it was because he had done his training as a junior doctor in the hospital and also because he lived locally in the area. To make matters worse, the Chairlady of the interviewing committee, in questioning me about my experience, asked me if I had ever operated on a perforated duodenal ulcer. It was like asking an accountant being interviewed for a job in a bank if he could count up to ten!

Soon after the latter experience, two events occurred that raised my morale and brought happiness to Eileen and me. The first was the birth of our eldest son, Terence. The second, which was to have an important bearing on my future career as a surgeon, was a phone call from my erstwhile Senior Medical Officer in Malaya. He had returned from Malaya. He enquired how I was enjoying civilian life and how my career in surgery was progressing. He told me that I should think about applying to return to the Army as a Regular Officer, as he felt I would have a worthwhile career as a surgeon in the Armed Forces. I was very reluctant to rejoin the Army. I felt that serving as a single officer was one thing, being married with a wife and child to care for was another, bearing in mind the turbulence of moving from one military hospital to another, possibly every few years, and the effect that would have on Eileen and on the education of our children, etc.

After further phone calls, during which I displayed my reluctance to apply for a Regular Commission, he offered me a position as a civilian surgeon, on a temporary basis, working in a military hospital in Germany, which he felt would give me the opportunity to get to know at firsthand what life in the Regular Army would be like, from the point of view of a medical officer and his family. I accepted his offer. Shortly after that, I was travelling back to London by road in extremely dense fog. I was second in a long line of cars, travelling very slowly, when I suddenly came to a halt and realised I had followed the car in front of me to its destination, the backyard of a butcher's shop. It occurred to me at the time that this incident symbolised the sudden end to my endeavours to develop a career in civilian life.

Mention of the end of my career in civilian life brought to my mind that as a surgeon I would no longer be addressed as Mr. I then wondered why surgeons were addressed as Mr. My visit to the butchers yard reminded me of what I had read somewhere about the answer to that question! Apparently, in years gone by when surgery was a more fearsome and unhygienic procedure, it was the habit of one London hospital to enlist the services of a butcher from nearby Smithfield market whose expertise in sawing through animal bones was valued when the occasion arose to sever those of humans. The assumption of 'Mr.' continued in usage when the latter function had become exclusively that of surgeons!

Chapter 8

Return to Service Life

In December 1953, I commenced working in the British Military Hospital in Rinteln. To begin with I lived in the Officers' Mess and Eileen went to Cork to stay with her father, who was ill. She and Terence joined me in Rinteln in late January. Rinteln is a small market town in northwest Germany. The hospital, which was located in an old German Army barracks, was situated only a short distance from the town. It had 200 beds and all the specialists and facilities of a District General Hospital, including ENT, Eye and Obs & Gyn departments.

Rinteln – view from our house.

48

The CO was well-liked and popular with his staff. He was one of the old school of gentlemen, a man of great integrity but who was always kind and considerate. He had a special interest in seeing that his staff and their families enjoyed a good social life.

We lived in a fine detached residence, and Rinteln being in one of the prettier parts of Lower Saxony, we had a landscape of rolling hills to be viewed from our house. Eileen enjoyed our stay in Rinteln very much. She had a full-time German maid, and there were good shopping facilities available, including a large NAAFI, and amenities, such as a horse-riding school which she regularly attended.

There were two incidents that occurred and caused me some anxiety and consternation. One was an injury to my son Terence. We had a large garden at the back of our house. When we took over the house, the grass in the garden had become very much overgrown, and to remedy this situation, we allowed a German shepherd bring his sheep into it and graze on it from time to time. One day, when Terence was playing with the sheepdog, it unfortunately bit him on his lip. The wound was very deep and nasty. Apart from the worry about the injury he sustained, there was

Sheepdog in our garden.

also the concern I felt about the possibility that the dog could be rabid. However, my mind was set at rest, when I looked at a photograph, that had been taken on a previous day, of Terence standing in the garden with the dog. The picture gave no indication that the dog was rabid, and taking into account the evidence I collected of its behaviour on the day Terence was bitten, I decided that Terence should not be given a course of antirabic inoculations, which would be quite prolonged, painful, and debilitating. Being the only surgeon available at that time, I also had the unenviable task of having to repair the damage to my son's lip. However, all went well, and he wasn't left with an unsightly scar.

The other incident occurred when a Russian Military Mission vehicle caught fire and the driver was severely burnt. He was brought to our hospital. He was accompanied by two Russian officers. When the officers were informed that the patient would have to have toilet of his burns carried out under general anaesthesia, they only gave their consent on being assured that they could be present in the operating theatre when the procedure was carried out. The next morning, they removed the chocolates and cigarettes that had been given to him by the nursing staff, saying that a Russian soldier did not need luxuries of that sort. They informed us that they had sent for an ambulance to take the patient to a hospital in East Berlin. In spite of being told that he was not fit to be moved, they insisted on moving him. After consultation with our CO and higher authority, it was agreed that there was nothing we could do, under the circumstances, to stop them taking him away.

Occasionally I had to visit German hospitals, with a view to arranging the transfer of an injured serviceman to our hospital. The soldier sustained his injuries either in a road traffic accident or when on an exercise. I regret to say that, presumably, since it was not long since the War ended, the German doctors had some catching up to do, with the advances we had made in the treatment of shock resulting from blood loss. Whilst our management of the casualty with significant blood loss was to transfuse urgently and adequately, they treated such cases on the assumption that they were suffering from a form of neurogenic shock and consequently used blood transfusion sparingly. In some cases they would amputate a limb, rather than transfuse, in the sincere belief that this procedure would reduce the severity of shock and indeed be life saving. It is, therefore, true to say that my visits to these hospitals were by and large in the nature of rescue missions.

I had an interesting experience, when I was requested to see the daughter of a senior officer. She was a very beautiful young lady, and was a high-class model, who was well-known in the world of ladies' fashions. Her father was concerned about the treatment she was having from her German doctor for phlebitis of her leg. He was treating the condition with the application of leeches to her leg! No doubt in the distant past this form of therapy was sound and rational, but it had in modern times been replaced by a more aesthetic and refined form of treatment.

From the point of view of the surgery I performed, it was more or less similar to what I was accustomed to in civilian life, a good deal of emergency surgery most of which had to do with trauma, and sufficient major cold surgery of an interesting and varied character.

In April 1955 another happy event occurred, namely the birth of my son, Fergus.

Reverting back to our esteemed CO, I felt very sorry for him, when things went wrong for him during the inspection of the hospital by a senior medical officer. The officer who was very thorough and efficient, found two patients sharing the same glass to drink from. He immediately demanded to be taken to the Quartermasters Department where he questioned the NCO in charge about the shortage of glasses. The NCO explained how he had lent the Officers' Mess the previous night some glasses for their cocktail party. This information did not impress the inspecting officer. However, the CO, in order to take the officer's mind away from the latter distressing incident, gave him a somewhat difficult problem to resolve. It concerned a patient, an officer's wife, who was always complaining about the treatment she was receiving. She would invariably remark that she was being treated like the wife of a private soldier! The officer very quickly redressed her grievance by informing her that he was immensely pleased to hear she was being treated as another rank's wife, for the reason that one of his main ambitions in life was to see that the wife of a private soldier got the best treatment that was available.

After I had spent a year in Rinteln, I felt I had to decide where my future lay, i.e., was it to be in civilian life or in the Army? Looking back at my surgical training in civilian life, I found that it was unique in that it allowed me to accumulate a very wide and varied experience of emergency surgery in general. Unlike the general surgeon in civilian practice, the surgeon in the Army had to be capable of undertaking emergency surgery in a much wider field, including the field of trauma, for example, opening the head and chest, and the management of soft tissue, bone and joint injuries, in his care of the serviceman and his family stationed outside the UK and in his role as a surgeon in time of war. In addition, the military surgeon has to have knowledge and experience of muscu-loskeletal conditions, which is outside the domain of the civilian general surgeon, and which may effect the serviceman's performance of his duties.

Having given this matter much thought, I felt that a surgical career in the Army would be very interesting and rewarding. I had sufficient experience of service life to know that my family would be happy and well looked after living in an Army environment. The facilities for the education of my children would be good. Above all else, Eileen had enjoyed serving for some years as a QARANC Officer and she was very pleased with our joint decision that I should seek a Regular Commission in the Army. In due course, I applied for the Commission and, subsequently, having attended the Army Officers Selection Board at the Ministry of Defence, I was pleased to be informed that my application was successful.

Back into Uniform

Upon being appointed to a Regular Commission, I was given the rank of Major. To save me the embarrassment of suddenly appearing in uniform

Hamburg.

in Rinteln, I was posted to the British Military Hospital in Hamburg, and this was in August 1955. The hospital was a well-constructed German hospital, purpose-built shortly before the War, and it was large, having accommodation for about 400 beds. It was very well equipped and staffed. Good relations between it and the local civilian hospitals were well-established, and maintained to the extent that a German surgeon was contracted to do relief duties for the senior surgeon at the military hospital.

We were given a fine old detached house to live in, situated in a quiet suburb not far from the hospital and we were very happy and contented living there. Hamburg had large areas which were devastated during the War, and had not yet been rebuilt. It was otherwise a beautiful city and its inhabitants were very friendly and good-natured.

I was not very busy. The highlight of my clinical work concerned the calls I received to see and treat patients in a small Service hospital some hours away, travelling there by road. Two of these cases spring to mind. One was a young girl who was run over by a vehicle. She had sustained a rupture of her diaphragm, which, fortunately, I was able to repair. The other was an infant with a congenital obstruction to the outlet of her stomach. These cases caused me a great deal of anxiety because I couldn't be available much after their operations to look after them. However, fortunately, there were very good doctors on the staff of the hospital who cared for them exceedingly well.

Regrettably, my relationship, at one time, with the CO became rather strained. In writing a routine confidential report on me, he stated that I needed some training and experience in the field of administration and recommended that I be posted to a Medical Reception Station as Officer i/c. I appealed against his recommendation on the grounds that I believed that I was fully capable of doing the administration connected with the running of my surgical unit, and that furthermore, and in any case, I came into the Army to undertake surgical duties and not administration. As a result of my appeal, the comments concerning administration were withdrawn from the report.

Talking of administration reminds me of the activities of our youngish Administration Officer, which could be considered to be beyond the call of duty. He was a very efficient officer who ran a form of social services for the staff of the hospital. He was known to some as 'Mr Fix It'. He seemed to have various contacts amongst the local civilians and, as a result, could arrange for things to be bought or sold, particularly cars, at reasonable prices. However, I hasten to add, there was nothing illegal or dishonest in his transactions.

In May 1956 my daughter, Finola, was born. She was born on a Sunday. When we returned from Mass that morning, I departed by helicopter to see a severely injured soldier in a German hospital some distance north of Hamburg. Eileen, when I departed, was feeling well and she was not expected to go into labour for at least another six weeks. However, a few hours later, I received a phone call in the German hospital from her obstetrician, informing me that it was necessary for her to have an emergency Caesarean Section and that he could not delay the operation until I returned. The patient I had come to see had a very serious head injury. Unfortunately, having discussed his case with a neurosurgeon in London on the phone, it was apparent that there was nothing in the way of operative surgical intervention that would aid his recovery. I returned to Hamburg and was pleased to find Eileen making a good recovery from her operation, and that our daughter was coping well with being born prematurely. This happy event was shortly afterwards followed by a tragic one, which affected me personally, namely the death of my brother, John . He, like me, was a surgeon.

Chapter 9

The Suez Campaign

In early August 1956, when I had just completed a year on duty in Hamburg and Finola was two months old, I received a posting order, requesting me to return immediately to the UK with my family. I was to be taken on the strength of a General Hospital, as Officer i/c Surgical Division, with the rank of Lt. Colonel. The hospital was being mobilised for the Suez Campaign, which was pending. This was my first insight into the effects the exigencies of the services may have on one's family. Whilst I journeyed to Chester to join the TA & VR General Hospital there, Eileen and our three young children travelled to Dublin, to live in a house Eileen had rented.

The Administrative Officer and I were the only Regular Army officers on the staff of the hospital. The remainder of the staff were either TA & VR personnel, or Reservists called back to the colours. I regret to say that there was a fault in the system that kept an up-to-date record of Reservists. The wife of one of them received a telegram calling him back to duty, when in fact he had been deceased for a number of years. In another case, the reservist had had his leg amputated a number of years previously! However, when our mobilisation was completed, we had a very fine nucleus of highly qualified and experienced specialists from civilian hospitals and I felt proud and honoured to be a member of the staff of the hospital. Our immediate destination was Cyprus. We flew out there in two Britannia aircraft from London airport. Our hospital equipment had already, in advance of our departure, gone by sea to meet up with us in Cyprus. Upon our arrival in Cyprus, we were located to begin with in a school building in Limasol. Much to our consternation, the school building was very isolated and insecure from an attack by Eoka terrorists, who were very active at that time. I am pleased to say that after a few days, we

Standing outside our Military Hospital in Cyprus.

moved into a new hospital that had not yet been occupied. It was more secure and could be easily guarded. Soon after we moved into the hospital, the ship transporting our equipment arrived. However, presumably as a result of our impatience to have our equipment unloaded as quickly as possible, we received a field laundry by mistake! Eventually, we received our own. It was at the bottom of the ship's hold.

Our final destination was thought to be the Palace Hotel in Port Said, where we would be located as the Base Hospital for the campaign. However, the war lasted only ten days and, consequently, we were never called upon to fulfil our real role in the campaign. Furthermore, the casualties were being evacuated from Suez, either to a Field Surgical Unit at sea on board an aircraft carrier, or were transported by air to Cyprus. The airport in Cyprus receiving the casualties was located not far from the permanently based military hospital on the island. As a result, we received only those casualties that were evacuated by sea, and they were few in number. However, I believe we did treat the first casualty of the war, so to speak, a French paratrooper who developed appendicitis just before he embarked for Suez.

To take the pressure off the garrison military hospital, which now had to deal with the Suez casualties as well as the islands terrorists' casualties, we were requested to undertake the treatment of the latter casualties, and as a result we became quite busy. As time went on, we became committed to also giving assistance to the surgeons in the local civilian hospital. We had many serious injuries to deal with. A young terrorist had serious wounds involving his head, chest, liver and kidney. Having made a good recovery from his injuries, he was later charged with the murder of a lawyer and faced the death penalty. Another case concerned a Cypriot judge who was shot and severely wounded by a terrorist. He was admitted to a private clinic, which was run by a Cypriot surgeon and his wife, who were suspected of being sympathisers with Eoka. I was requested by the security forces to go to the clinic and render assistance in the treatment of

Nicosia.

his injuries. When I arrived at the clinic, such was the concern felt for the safety of the judge, I found it surrounded by the security forces. After entering the building, our anaesthetist, who was accompanying me, and I were taken to the operating theatre, where we found the patient was already being prepared for his operation. The surgeon agreed to the Army anaesthetist giving the anaesthetic and to me assisting him at the operation. The patient had a very severe abdominal injuries. We fortunately had brought some blood with which to resuscitate him. Regrettably, the surgeon's operative surgical technique was slow and too meticulous, to put it simply, to suit the urgency of the situation. In spite of my efforts to speed things up, he continued to operate at a slow pace and I regret very much to have to report that the patient died before the operation was completed. When I look back, it is easy for me to see with the aid of hindsight, that the patient's best chance of survival would have been for him to have been evacuated to our Military Hospital as soon as his resuscitation had been completed.

Our most notable casualty was the Commander of a French battleship who, on his way back to France after the cessation of the hostilities, decided to come ashore at Limassol, and pay his respects to the RN Flag Officer stationed on the island. Regrettably, shortly after he came ashore, the jeep he was travelling in was blown up by a terrorist land-mine. He sustained serious leg injuries, which amounted mainly to an open fracture of his shin bone. The management of these injuries is staged, the first stage being the toilet and debridement of the wound, and the next stage, the closure of the wound five or six days later. Having completed the initial treatment phase of his injuries, I, on the following morning, was explaining to him, with the aid or an interpreter, his staff officer, what the next stage of his treatment would be, when the latter officer interrupted me and pointed out to me that the Commandant's ship was returning to its French naval base that day, and that it was French naval tradition that a ship never, if possible, returns to its base without its Commandant. In spite of the British Army Commander's attempts to persuade him not to leave, a helicopter from his ship duly arrived that day and evacuated him back to his ship. In truth, I was not very concerned about his early return to France, since in a war situation the initial treatment I had given him would have been equivalent to what he would have received in a Casualty Clearing Station, and it would have been quickly followed by his evacuation to a General or even Base Hospital.

As time went on, it must become apparent to the 'powers that be' that our hospital personnel were no longer engaged in the role they were mobilised for, and that consequently they were anxious to return to their civilian occupations. Shortly before Christmas 1956 we returned to the UK. On the day before we left Cyprus, we were accommodated in Nicosia, in preparation for our departure from the airport there. I remembered that I had not bought any Christmas presents to bring home to my family. I hired a taxi to take me to the main shopping centre. As we entered the main street of the city, my driver stopped the taxi and declared that he wasn't prepared to proceed any further. I was completely ignorant of the reasons for his action. I walked down the street in full uniform and did my shopping. That night, I had a visit from the Military Police, who informed me that I had done my shopping in a street that was out of bounds to British servicemen and that it was called the 'murder mile' because of the number of people who had been killed by terrorists there. They also declared that I had by my presence there committed a Court Martial offence. However, since I was leaving the island on the following day, they were prepared to forego charging me with the offence.

Chapter 10

Return to Germany

Upon my return to the UK, I was posted to BMH Hannover, and after a period of disembarkation leave, I proceeded to Germany in February 1957. We lived in a flat for a short while and then moved into a very nice house in an Army cantonment.

During my tour of duty in Hannover, a good deal of my time was spent visiting German hospitals, with a view to transferring, as soon as possible, servicemen who had been admitted to them, to our Military Hospital. As already mentioned in a previous chapter, we were concerned about the standard of primary care of casualties in German hospitals, particularly from the point of view of the reluctance to give blood transfusions to casualties suffering from shock due to blood loss. It seemed to me that their management of shock in trauma care was influenced to a large extent by their belief in neurogenic shock, resulting from the effects of injury stresses on the nervous system, being an important form of shock in the severely injured. I felt that the shortcomings of the German doctors in this respect was due to the disruption of their medical schools by the effects of the War and also to the fact that towards the end of the War, as a matter of necessity, medical students were being qualified as doctors before they had completed their final year in medical school. However, I am pleased to record that when I visited Germany some years later, their treatment standards were very high and they had made great advances in medical skills and technology, which were highly regarded. For the reasons I have just mentioned, my visits to German hospitals were often a matter of some urgency and, as a result, I invariably used a helicopter for transportation. I had a very extensive area of northwest Germany to cover. It extended right up to the Baltic coast. I had many interesting experiences. I recall the occasion when I was returning from a small town on the Baltic coast, the pilot of my helicopter informed me that we were running short of fuel. Feeling that a large Army unit he had spotted in open countryside might let him have some fuel, he decided to land close by. However, as we were landing, a German police officer appeared as if from nowhere and ordered us to move away as quickly as possible. It appeared that we were landing on an artillery firing range and at any moment, the firing would commence! We then flew along the coast and came across a small German naval base. The German naval officers appeared, for some reason, to be embarrassed by our presence and directed us to the docks at Bremerhaven, which weren't far away, and where we succeeded in getting fuel.

Soon after I had arrived in Hannover, I was introduced to an honorary civilian member of our Officers' Mess. He was an ex-British serviceman. I observed that he had a constant drip from his nose. I had already heard from another member of the Mess that he had suffered from serious head injuries when he was involved in a motor car accident about a year previously. Linking his nasal 'drip' to his history of a severe head injury made me surmise that he was suffering from a very serious complication of his head injury, namely a cerebrospinal fistula. The latter complication meant that, as a result of a fracture of his skull, a communication had been established between the layer of fluid, i.e., the cerebrospinal, surrounding his brain, and his nose. This complication could, at any time, result in very serious consequences, namely meningitis. Having discussed what I presumed to be the cause of his nasal 'drip' with him, and its treatment, a major neurosurgical operation, I then proceeded to tell him that I could arrange for the operation to be done by a neurosurgeon in London, if his own doctor and his wife wished me to do so. However, his wife, soon afterwards, rang to tell me she wanted the operation carried out in Germany, and that his doctor was arranging for him to be admitted to a clinic in Cologne. The German neurosurgeon performing the operation invited me to be present at it.

I was most impressed with his operative technique. The operation was expertly performed indeed. After the operation, the neurosurgeon told me that as soon as the patient was fit to leave the hospital, he would be sent to a 'Spa' to convalesce. I enquired about the rationale of convalescing in a 'Spa'. He stated that, during the operation the patient would have sustained a certain degree of 'commotio cerebri' or concussion of the brain, which would result in some lowering of his blood pressure and slowing of his pulse. The therapy he would receive in the 'Spa', i.e., hot and cold baths, physical exercises, etc. would reverse the effects of the concussion. I felt that we had descended from the sublime to the ridiculous! Not unexpectedly, the patient, after a few days in the 'Spa', frantically phoned me, and requested me to take him home, as he couldn't stand anymore of the rigorous treatment he was having. However, I hasten to add, when he did return home, he made an excellent recovery from his operation, which indeed was a great success.

The visit of our Command Director of Medical Services had its humorous side to it. When he visited our Pschyciatric ward, he walked down the line of patients standing at the foot of their beds, and spoke a few encouraging words to each patient. However, the last in line was a bearded RN able-bodied seaman. The inspecting officer extolled the virtures of the Senior Service to him, and then remarked to him, 'My good fellow, you must be very proud to be serving in the Royal Navy.' The patient replied, 'If you feel that way about the RN, why the bloody hell, didn't you join it yourself!'

On a more depressing note was the occasion Eileen and I visited the former concentration camp at Belsen. What remained of the camp was very eerie and desolate. The most striking feature was the large mounds of earth, where the mass graves of thousands of the inmates had been. Strangely enough, there were no birds to be seen, and no flowers were blooming, on that beautiful spring day of our visit.

In contrast, was our visit to Hameln, where every Sunday morning, the play *The Pied Piper of Hameln* was enacted. It was indeed a more joyful occasion.

'Pied Piper of Hameln'.

In 1958, a good deal of publicity, very favourable to us I hasten to add, was given in the German press (headline – 'British Doctors Save The Life of German Sergeant') to the treatment we gave to a German soldier who had sustained injuries when on a training exercise. Because of the life-threatening nature of his injuries, he was brought direct to our Military Hospital by helicopter. Happily, he made a good recovery from his injuries. The reason for the notoriety his case received, I suspect, was that arguably, he must have been one of the first German soldiers to be treated in a British Military Hospital since the War ended.

We had an interesting, if not a trying, experience when my family and I went by train to Italy for a holiday. At Innsbruck, the Austrian immigration officers discovered that Eileen's passport was a few days out of date. They let us continue our journey into Italy however, and told us that we shouldn't have any problems entering Italy. Little did we know what was to be in store for us when we reached the Italian frontier station. As I looked out on the platform, I could see two men in mufti looking into each carriage as they walked down the platform. When they came to our compartment, they immediately boarded the train. It looked as if they had been warned by their colleagues in Austria about our out-of-date passport, and consequently were on the lookout for us. We were taken off the train

Our holiday in Venice.

and escorted by the two men into an office. An officer seated at a desk, having inspected our passports, informed us that since Eileen's passport was out of date, she couldn't enter Italy. I pleaded with him, mentioning that her passport was only a few days out of date, and that I was a British Army officer, but to no avail. I then remembered that Eileen's uncle was the Irish Ambassador to Italy. I said I wished to make a phone call to the Irish Ambassador's office in Rome, and told the immigration officer of Eileen's relationship to the Ambassador. This caused the officer to become conciliatory and friendly. After a discussion with his colleagues, he informed us that we could continue our journey into Italy. He also issued us with an exit visa for our return journey.

During our stay in Hannover, one day, when driving my car, an incident occurred that could have ended tragically. My son, Terence, was sitting in the front passenger seat when the door on his side suddenly flew open. Terence fell sideways through the open door and, as he was falling, I managed with one hand to grab hold of his foot. Unfortunately, his shoe came off in my hand and he fell to the ground. There was a fair amount of traffic on the road, but fortunately he was not run over as he lay on the ground. I was also concerned about him being run over by the rear wheel of my car, and to avoid that happening, I instinctively, at the crucial moment, turned the car away from his side of the road. This resulted in the car almost colliding with a lamppost. Fortunately, we were not far away from my hospital, and I immediately drove him there. His injuries to begin with were considered to be very serious, but, however, after a period of observation, it was concluded that he had sustained only a fracture of a rib and severe bruising and abrasions.

I spent one particular trying time when I was treating a young officer with very serious leg injuries. His father was a senior General. Soon after I had completed the initial phase of the treatment of his injuries, there was an outcry from higher authority, including MOD, to have the patient brought back to the UK for high-powered specialist treatment there. I was not inclined to agree to have my patient transferred to another unit at what was a vital stage in his treatment. It so happened just then, that his father came to see him. He was pleased with his son's progress and the treatment he was receiving. He intimated to me that he did not wish to have his son moved to the UK until I felt it was necessary. Regrettably the patient subsequently developed a very serious complication, namely, the widespread dissemination of fat emboli from his fracture, a condition which could be lethal. Fortunately, in due course, he made a good recovery from the complication, and from then on progressed well.

I had one 'brush' with the German police. A traffic police officer stuck a document on the windscreen of my car. My car was parked outside my house in the Army cantonment where we lived. The document stated that I had contravened a traffic regulation by parking my car where I did, and that I was to report to the local police station. When I entered the police station, I was ushered into an office. I handed the document to a police officer sitting behind a desk. Having read the document, he immediately stood up, clicked his heels, and started to speak to me in German, and in such a tone of voice that I got the impression he was reading the Riot Act to me! When he finished his tirade, I asked him if he spoke English. He replied that he spoke a little English. I then tried to explain to him that I lived in an Army cantonment, but it was to no avail. Fortunately, his superior officer then entered the room. He spoke good English, and immediately realised that a mistake had been made. After he made some very uncomplimentary remarks to his colleague, he turned to me and apologised for his colleagues stupidity, and for the ordeal I had been put through.

After spending three years in Hannover, I was posted to the British Military Hospital in Iserlohn in March 1960. Iserlohn is a small town, not far from Dortmund, and indeed from the Dutch border. In those days, the function of the hospital was to care for the sick and wounded of the Canadian Brigade, which had its base in that area. The hospital was to a large extent staffed with Canadian medical officers and nursing officers. The hospital was quite busy. A good deal of the surgical workload had to do with servicemen being involved in road traffic accidents. My deputy, a young Canadian surgeon, was a workaholic and seemed to be always looking for more work to do. One Saturday morning, when he happened to be walking behind a patient who was on his way out of the hospital, having had a fairly major operation, he spotted a large sebaceous cyst on the back of the patient's neck. I might add that these cysts are innocent cysts which do not require urgent surgery. However, he arranged for the cyst to be removed before the patient was discharged. Subsequently, the patient, in his endeavours to leave the hospital before any other problem might arise and prevent his discharge, by mistake joined a queue of patients awaiting to be examined, following treatment of minor conditions which were mainly piles. Three weeks later, when he attended my outpatients clinic, he complimented my surgical unit for being so thorough in its examination of patients prior to their discharge from hospital, and mentioned his experience of being examined 'from top to bottom'.

During our sojourn in Iserlohn, we were fortunate in having Winterburg winter holiday resort within easy driving distance. During one of our visits to the resort, I decided to learn to ski. I joined a ski school run by an Austrian instructor. On the first morning I attended the school, I had an unfortunate experience. It took some time for me to be fitted out with my ski kit and, as I made my way to the class, I, realising that I was going to be late in joining it, became frantic. Eventually, I found myself skiing down out of control, in the direction of the class, which was lined up facing down a nursery slope. To my horror, I collided with the class and caused the class to collapse like a pack of cards. Fortunately, no one was injured. The instructor was very annoyed with me and left me in no doubt what he thought of me. After a hurried demonstration of the 'snow plough', he ordered me to ski down the nursery slopes and show the class how it was done. Needless to say, I soon fell off my skis and tumbled down to the bottom of the slope. Feeling very embarrassed, I quickly got up and immediately made my way back to our hostel. Later that morning, I went down to the bar. As I was about to have a drink, a very irate officer entered the bar and, standing some distance from me, said something to the barman in an angry tone of voice. I asked the barman who he was and what was he angry about. He told me that he was the Army Commander and that he was telling him what he would do to the officer who knocked him off his skis when he attended the ski instruction class that morning. My response to this disturbing piece of information was to hurriedly and surreptitiously vacate the bar and return to my room.

I had an interesting experience, when I acted as a surgical adviser to the Prosecuting Officer at a Court Martial. A young serviceman was being tried for the murder of a German civilian. He had stamped on the head of the civilian with his boot in a fracas. The latter individual died some days later in hospital. A young lawyer in London, who some years later became a renowned QC, undertook the defence of the soldier. On perusing the deceased's hospital case records, he observed that the victim had had a fever for a few days before he died. At the Court Martial, a famous London forensic pathologist in giving evidence for the prosecution, stated that the deceased had sustained a fracture of his skull, which had extended into a sinus, and as a result, had developed meningitis, which ultimately caused his death. However, a senior Army pathologist, who was in attendance with me, and I, towards the end of the Court Martial proceedings, reviewed the medical evidence that had been presented. We found in the deceased's medical records, a pathological report on the examination of his cerebospinal fluid that had not been presented to the Court. The findings in the latter report, were not in keeping with what one would expect to find in a case of meningitis resulting from a fracture of the skull, according to what we found recorded in a well-recognised textbook on Diseases of the Nervous System. We submitted the aforementioned pathological report to the Court. The Defence Council, as a result, made the plea, that there was significant doubt about the victim having died from meningitis as a result of his injury. The findings of the Court Martial, subsequently, were that the accused was guilty of manslaughter.

Chapter 11

Return to the Far East

In March 1961 I was posted to Singapore as consultant Surgeon and officer i/c Surgical division in the Military Hospital. We spent three years in Singapore. Our children accompanied us and attended Army schools there, where the standard of education was high and left nothing to be desired. We lived in a large colonial house not far from the sea and as a result we had the benefit of cool breezes which together with wide open windows and ceiling fans made the heat bearable indoors.

British Military Hospital, Singapore.

Our house in Singapore.

The Hospital had a tragic history. It was invaded by Japanese soldiers during the last World War. Many of its patients and staff were killed including some in the operating theatre. It was very large, having about 400 beds, and was well staffed with specialists and well-equipped.

My previous experience of serving in the Far East had to do with the treatment of casualties from the Malayan Terrorist Campaign. The respite from war surgery did not last long. To begin with, a rebellion occurred in Brunei in December 1962. Fortunately it was very quickly squashed. It was of such a low key in gaining momentum, that the Field Surgical Team we sent there were able to hire a taxi to take them to the civilian hospital from the airport at Brunei. However soon afterwards, the Borneo campaign commenced with the infiltration of Indonesians from Indonesian Borneo into Eastern Malaysia. The casualties were evacuated from Borneo to our hospital in Singapore after receiving primary care in civilian hospitals. However, as the fighting increased it became my duty to go to Kuching and site a Field Surgical Team there. I sited the team in the civilian hospital. Evacuation of the casualties from the fighting areas in the jungle was directly to the civilian hospital by helicopter. Incidentally

Kuching in those days was a beautiful garden city and after arranging for the siting of the surgical team I spent a pleasant few days there.

I had another interesting experience when I was requested to go to Nepal to see our surgeon in the British Military Hospital there who was ill. The hospital was situated in Dharan, a small town in the foothills of the Himalayas in East Nepal. It provided medical care for Gurkha soldiers newly recruited, and for pensioners and their families on their return home following military service. Large numbers of civilians, Nepalese, some of whom had walked for days or even weeks to reach the hospital, were also cared for. The hospital was purpose-built and modern and had 70 beds. It had a small staff of British Army doctors and nurses. The medical staff consisted of a surgeon, anaesthetist, physician and the commanding officer who was a medical officer. A laboratory, X-ray department and dispensary were run by senior RAMC technicians. Specialists in various fields from the UK, Singapore and Hong Kong visited the hospital on a regular basis. The medical conditions the hospital had to deal with included trauma, tetanus, chronic bone infection, neglected burns, tuberculosis in many forms and malignant disease.

My journey to Nepal was quite eventful. Having flown to Calcutta I stayed overnight there in a high-class old colonial-style hotel. The accommodation in my hotel contrasted vividly with what I was to see of the living conditions of the citizens of Calcutta who were homeless, when I walked about the city. The homeless were living in hovels which in most cases were tiny shacks with their roofs made of newspapers and which were large enough only for their inhabitants to crawl in and out of on their hands and knees. From the number of times I was accosted on the streets, it was apparent that these unfortunate people depended on begging for their livelihood. The next morning I embarked on my train journey to Nepal. When I arrived at my departure station in Calcutta with a Gurkha Sgt. who was to accompany me on my journey, I was met by an individual who wore the uniform of a stationmaster. He bowed down before me and exclaimed, 'Sahib, I always look after British Officer very well. Come with me. I have special sleeping compartment for you. In the morning when train reaches the Ganges river you need not get up as the part of the train I have put you and the Sgt. in will cross the river.' I thanked him for his kindness and handed him a large tip. His response to my generosity was to bow very low and mutter something about me being a great British Officer. He then quickly departed and as he did so the Gurkha Sgt. turned to me and said that he was a 'bad man' and that he was not the Stationmaster! When we entered our compartment we found only a tier of two wooden planks in it. Worse was to come. When we reached the Ganges there was no train ferry to take us across the river in our compartment. Like every one else we left the train and crossed the river in a passenger ferry boat and boarded a train on the other side of the river. My next surprise came when we stopped at a station and a waiter dressed in a clean white uniform appeared at our carriage window announcing breakfast was being served. I was in the process of ordering bacon and egg when my Gurkha companion intervened and cancelled my order. He then led me on to the platform and showed me the improvised kitchen that had been set up to cook our meal. To my horror, I could see that dishes were being washed by dipping them into a dirty and filthy bucket of water. I settled for an orange for breakfast. As we continued our journey, I observed, that after we pulled out of a station the train would slow down to allow a large number of people waiting on the side of the track to clamber on to it. Some of these people would travel holding on to the sides of a carriage and others would sit on its roof. Coming to a tunnel the train would slow down almost coming to a halt to allow the clandestine passengers to alight! One could only assume that this unusual form of rail travel was undertaken at the behest of a special code of conduct of the train drivers

Crossing the Ganges.

union. Before we reached our destination, an unpleasant incident occurred, which, thanks to the good auspices of my Gurkha friend, did not have any untoward consequences. As we sat at the end of a long bench in our compartment, a group of young men who were sitting alongside of us started to become hostile towards us and attempted to push us off the end of the bench. The Gurkha Sgt. immediately stood up and removed his kukri from his bag. He then proceeded to brandish the weapon in front of them and in Gurkhali promised them a long life in another world. They became very cowed and rushed off the train when we reached the next station. We subsequently completed our train journey at Beratnager, a town near the Nepalese border. From there we made our way, a short journey, by road in a jeep to Dharan.

I was pleased when I arrived to be informed that the surgeon was well on his way to making a good recovery from his illness. After spending a few days visiting the hospital and standing in for the surgeon whilst he was recovering, I prepared to make my return journey to Singapore. Regrettably, on the morning of my departure, the anaesthetist was found to be missing. He had not returned from a short trek he had made into the hills the previous evening. I cancelled my arrangements for departure.

Mount Everest on Christmas morning.

Fortunately he was soon found by a search party in a rest station on top of one of the foothills. He was suffering from a form of depression brought on by a prolonged tour of duty in such an isolated part of the world. I am glad to say, that after a few days rest from duty and the assurance that he would soon be returning to the UK, he recovered well from his illness. However by that time it was Christmas Eve. On the morning of Christmas Day, I trekked into the foothills, and from there, I had the pleasure of, in the distance, seeing Mount Everest when the clouds obscuring its peak disappeared for a few moments. A few days later I returned to Singapore by air from Bertnarger via Calcutta. Incidentally my journey to Calcutta was in an old Nepalese Dakota aircraft in which the passengers were accompanied by their livestock e.g., goats and chickens, etc.

Part of my work in Singapore was to do with doing relief duties for surgeons in other hospitals. This commitment gave me the opportunity of returning to Nepal in December 1963. On this occasion travelling by air to Calcutta I had a stopover in Bangkok, which allowed me to see the magnificent Buddhist temples there. My journey north from Calcutta was uneventful apart from the sight of a man going beserk on a platform of a station we had stopped at. He was running up and down the platform

Temples in Bangkok.

threatening people with a knife he held in his outstretched hand. However, our train pulled out of the station before I could see what the outcome of his frenzy was going to be.

The two weeks I spent in Dharan were a unique and memorable experience. The clinical problems that presented in the hospital seldom were seen in the practice of medicine in our modern western civilisation, and one had to give a great deal of thought and consideration to their management. I greatly admired the medical and nursing staff of the hospital for the way they coped with the very large numbers of patients who arrived at the hospital seeking treatment. The hospital had not long been opened, and, as awareness of its existence spread, an ever-increasing number of Nepalese walked or were even carried over increasing distances sometimes for many weeks, seeking medical care. An innate suspicion of western-style medicine among the more isolated hill dwellers, resulted in patients attending the hospital as a last resort, they having consulted the local traditional healer in the first instance.

These patients, as mentioned previously, suffered from neglected burns, fractures, tuberculosis, congenital abnormalities and malignant conditions. In addition it was not unusual for them to sustain bear bites and

Patients waiting area outside the Military Hospital in Dharan.

snake bites. Some arrived at the hospital in the advanced stages of obstructed labour. Goitres were endemic and it was not unusual for patients to present with massive goitres. With the small number of beds that were available in the hospital, the large number of patients that arrived daily at the hospital gave the staff, when the hospital first opened, a considerable problem, a problem akin to that which might confront a medical officer when he has to deal with an overload of casualties on the battlefield. The solution to the problem was to site a reception or waiting area in the field outside the hospital, where the vetting of the patients was carried out. The vetting procedure, which was undertaken by an experienced Gurkha clerk, was in fact a system triage, a system which ensured that 'the most good was done for the most patients'. In other words, priority for attendance at the necessary out-patient clinic was given to those cases the hospital had the necessary resources i.e., medical skills, etc., to treat available, and in addition as a rule, priority was given to those patients requiring short-term bed occupancy. Those cases who were not seen at the clinic on a particular day would stay in the village of Dharan in the hope that they would be successful in their endeavours on another day. The principles of surgery we practise in western civilisation had in some ways to be amended in Nepal to suit the needs of the indigenous population there. Most of the Nepalese patients were hill dwellers. There was no transport to take them on their journeys. A good deal of their lifetime was spent climbing hills with heavy packs on their backs. They could frequently be seen carrying large collections of branches, cut down from the trees, which they used for thatching the roofs of their dwellings or for firewood. Consequently, from the functional point of view, they needed to be able to bend their hips and knees very well as they climbed the hills with heavy loads on their backs. Furthermore, when they rested indoors or outdoors on their travels, they sat on the ground. Unlike the patient in western civilisation, the Nepalese hill dweller, if he is to be left with a stiff hip or knee as a result of an injury or by design in the treatment of a joint condition, must have the joint preferably in a bent position. It is also interesting to note that the patients sustained their burns from the open fire they sited on the middle of the floor of their small dwellings and around which they sat at night. Their fractures were sustained usually from falling off trees they had climbed to collect firewood. The high incident of tuberculosis that presented was probably due to living in small overcrowded and poorly ventilated dwellings.

My two most memorable cases incidentally were a massive goitre and a huge ovarian cyst. The latter cyst occupied about half the patient's abdomen and after its removal, her heart stopped beating. Fortunately, however, we were able to revive her and she made a good recovery from her operation subsequently. I might add in contemplating my reminiscences of surgery in Nepal, I remember that there was a problem about giving a blood transfusion. We had to rely on the patient's relatives donating blood, and, unfortunately they very rarely agreed to donate it for reasons which were understandable. Towards the end of my short sojourn in Nepal, I had developed a high regard and love of its inhabitants.

On another occasion I was required to do a few weeks relief duties in Hong Kong. Our military hospital there was situated on top of Mount Kellet. I flew to Hong Kong in a small twin-engined cargo RAF aircraft. I sat with the crew in the cockpit of the plane. Because of the relatively low altitude we flew at, my journey to Hong Kong was a somewhat absorbing and unique experience. Our low altitude allowed the navigator to pick out landmarks, and consequently I got a picturesque view particularly of the coast of Vietnam with its panoramic background of jungle inland. However the serenity and tranquillity of the beauty of nature, I was observing below me, was suddenly disturbed by the appearance of a giant B52 American Air Force bomber aircraft crossing the coastline at a great height above us, and by the sight of plumes of smoke arising from the jungle in the far distance, presumably where the plane had dropped its bombs! We made a brief stop at Saigon airport for refuelling, but were not allowed to leave the runway whilst our plane was being refuelled.

That air journey to Hong Kong, incidentally, was in complete contrast to the occasion when I flew there in the RAF Commander's high-powered jet plane. Some of the instruments in the cockpit of the plane, such as those concerned with the speed and height of the aircraft, were duplicated in the Commander's cabin, and before we took off, the pilot entered the cabin and remarked to the Commander that he didn't want any backseat driving from him. On this occasion, we stopped overnight for refuelling at the Clark US Army air base in the Philippines.

During my stay in Hong Kong I found living on top of the Mount very restful and peaceful. The air was cool and very invigorating. The hospital was not busy and the nature and volume of my work was in complete contrast to what I had experienced in Nepal. I felt I needed the rest very badly and was pleased that, being the surgeon on call all the time I was there, I was constrained from doing any sightseeing in Hong Kong or the New Territories.

I subsequently returned to Singapore feeling refreshed and well-equipped both mentally and physically to deal with the stress of my work there. Looking back at the work I did, I can recall some very interesting but highly stressful cases I had to deal with. They included a child with a liver abscess, the aspiration of which produced a large round worm; the perforation of a patient's gullet by a fish bone; and the spread of the inflammation of a patient's pancreas into his lung.

Subsequently, when I explored the child's liver, I found several small abscesses in it. In each abscess, there was a 'nest' of small worms. Following the extirpation of the abscesses, the patient recovered well from her illness. As regards the patient who presented with the fish bone in his gullet, whilst the fish bone was easily removed endoscopically, an intricate and delicate operation had to be performed to locate and drain an abscess that had formed at the back of the gullet. The management of the case with the spread of a pancreatic abscess into his lung was based on the simple procedure of emptying a bath by removing its plug. Drainage of the abscess had already been established via an opening in the abdominal wall overlying it. However, the resultant drainage tract had, regrettably, become blocked. Simply dilating the tract by passing a bougie down it, a procedure akin to removing the plug from a bath, brought about free drainage of the tract right up to its extension in the lung and, eventually, complete resolution of the latter extension.

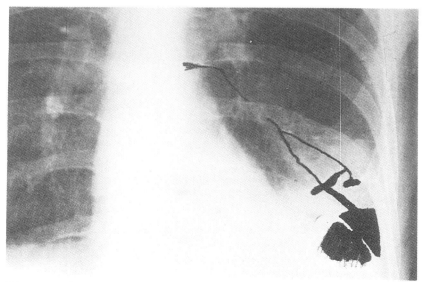

Diagrammatic representation of Pancreatic abscess spreading into lung.

Perhaps one of the most worrying and unfortunate cases was the young serviceman who was admitted as a result of a road traffic accident with a rupture of his Thoracic Aorta, the large artery in the chest arising from the heart. At the emergency operation, I was fortunate in being able to repair the damage done to the vessel wall by covering it with a sleeve of fascia taken from his chest wall. He recovered well from his operation. However, on the tenth day after the operation when he was about to be evacuated by air to the UK for more definitive repair of his damaged vessel, he suddenly collapsed from a secondary haemorrhage. I remembered that a cardiothoracic unit had just opened in the civilian General Hospital and after resuscitating my patient I transferred him to that unit, having alerted it to be ready to operate on him. Regrettably, the patient died during the operation, despite the heroic efforts of the unit's surgeons.

I had another case who died after severe chest injuries sustained in a road traffic accident in Malaya. This patient was the dear wife of a senior colleague of mine. I operated on her in the small military hospital she had been brought to after the accident, and subsequently evacuated her by helicopter to our hospital in Singapore. Regrettably, a short time later she suddenly collapsed and died.

Towards the end of my tour in Singapore I received the tragic news of the death of my father. Unfortunately, it was not possible for me to return to Ireland in time to attend his funeral.

During our sojourn in Singapore, we experienced two unsettling incidents. One was a burglary, when we lost a large amount of valuable jewellery and silverware. Regrettably, we didn't have the stolen property insured. The other unfortunate incident concerned the death of our mongrel dog which we had inherited from the previous occupants of our house. He had become very attached to the children and they to him, so much so, that he would accompany them in the mornings to the bus stop, which was some distance from our house, and would be waiting there when they returned in the afternoon. One morning, as they waited for the bus, the dog lay down in the middle of the road. To their horror, the bus, when it arrived, ran over the dog and killed it. Needless to say, my children were very shocked by the incident and were upset by it subsequently for some time.

Eileen and the children enjoyed their stay in Singapore very much. The amenities available to them were very good, and included a swimming pool, cinemas, golf, boat trips around the islands off Singapore, and holidays in the cool climate of the Cameron Highlands in Malaya or on the island of Penang. I myself had the enjoyment of playing golf fairly often on a course situated quite conveniently to the hospital, and to end this chapter on a humorous note, I will relate the story of one of the most embarrassing moments of my life.

In order to avoid the 'rush hour' of golfers wanting to play nine holes of golf before darkness set in the evenings, I and a colleague would hurry to the course, hoping to start our round before other golfers arrived. On one occasion, we arrived on the first tee perspiring and somewhat breathless from our endeavours. When I drove off, my club flew out of my hands, and ended up on top of a very tall tree, much to my dismay. My Malayan caddie immediately, and before I could stop him, started to climb the tree to retrieve my club. The tree was only about twenty yards from the tee. Very soon the tee was crowded with evening 'rush hour' gofers all intent on watching the caddie climb the tree. The caddie had a long way to go to reach the top of the tree and, as time went by, more and more people came to watch the spectacle. In due course the caddie retrieved my club, and I am pleased to say, subsequently descended safely to terra firma, by which time any further golf was abandoned for the day because of the light failing. The next day, the incident was prominently reported in the local newspaper. For sometime afterwards, whenever I entered the clubhouse, I felt that I was being pointed out by members to other members, as the person who put his no. one wood on top of the tree in front of the first tee!

Incidentally, my Surgical Wardmaster, a S/Sgt. was a keen golfer. At that time, an Army golf course had just been built. My S/Sgt. decided that he would play a round on it, and afterwards, report back to me, on what he thought of it. The next day, when I asked him how he got on with his round of golf, he replied in his broad Yorkshire accent, 'I came between Vicar and wife', and when I asked to explain what happened, he said, 'On one side of the first fairway, there is a long row of houses and when I sliced my ball off the tee, there was the sound of broken glass, followed by the appearance of a man with dog-collar outside a house, shouting that I had come between him and his wife as they were sitting having their breakfast!' He then went on to tell me that for the first time in his life he had lost a ball on a green, because of the height of the grass on it.

Chapter 12

Return to the UK

In April 1964 my family and I returned to the UK. After a period of disembarkation leave, I commenced duty in a Tidworth Military Hospital in Hampshire. We were given a large and very comfortable house to reside in. We had no difficulty in finding suitable schools for our children to attend. There was a town with good shopping facilities not far from where we lived. The hospital had 200 beds and was well-equipped and staffed with nurses and doctors, including specialists, to cope with its workload. It cared for the servicemen and their families in the local garrison and in the other garrisons throughout the south-west of England. It also had the very important role of treating the casualties from the training exercises on Salisbury plain. In addition, it accepted cases from the local GPs, and treated patients who sustained injuries in road traffic accidents locally. It was, it could be said, equivalent to a busy District General Hospital.

During the four years I spent working in this hospital, I involved myself in the work of two clinical projects. One of these projects concerned the introduction into my surgical practice of a new form of injection therapy for varicose veins that had at that time been developed. In order to learn as much as possible about the therapy, I offered myself as a patient for treatment of my own varicose veins to the specialist in a London hospital who had become an expert in the use of this procedure. After I received my injections, I was advised to walk about two miles a day for about six weeks, with the compression bandage that had been applied to my leg still being worn. At that time we had just purchased a cottage in the country-side. It so happened that there was a small village about a mile from our cottage. Fortunately it had a pub in it, and that gave me the incentive I needed, i.e., a pint of beer, to accomplish my objective of walking two miles each evening. I am pleased to say that the new form of therapy brought about a very good resolution of my varicose veins and that subsequently I developed my own vein clinic. However, I hasten to add, that on the other hand I did not become an alcoholic.

The other clinical project I became involved in was a research study in the surgical treatment of duodenal ulcers, i.e., Vagotomy. At that time, the principle of treating these ulcers by the reduction of acid in the stomach, with the surgical procedure of denerevation (i.e., Vagotomy), had become established. There were two ways of performing the operation, and there was a difference of opinion amongst surgeons about which procedure was the more effective way of reducing the output of acid in the stomach. My study was undertaken to determine which of the two procedures brought about the better reduction of acid. To enable me to carry out the study, I spent six months working in a London teaching hospital. My appraisal of the effects of the two procedures indicated that there was no significant difference between them in their potential for acid reduction. Subsequently, my university awarded me the degrees of MA, MD, for the thesis I produced on my research project.

Although I found my work very satisfying and rewarding, I had two very tragic events to cope with. One Saturday morning I said goodbye to the Commanding Officer as he set off on two weeks' holiday. On the following morning, much to my dismay, I received a telephone call informing me that he had died suddenly from a heart attack. As I was his second-in-command, I was requested by higher authority to assume command of the hospital immediately. One of the first tasks I had to undertake was to organise the funeral service of our late CO. He was, of course, to be buried with full military honours. It was the most stressful and exacting military duty I had had to perform so far in my army career.

I enjoyed being acting Commanding Officer very much. I was fortunate in having a Matron, an Administrative Officer, a Company Officer, an RSM, and a team of clinical specialists, who gave me their full support and allegiance. I hope I earned their respect in return for their loyalty to me. I believe I did. I endeavoured to lead always by giving a good example to others, being a good listener and by maintaining discipline in the unit with a firm hand but above all else with fairness. I was fortunate in being able to find enough time to run my surgical unit in addition to commanding the hospital. However, after commanding the hospital for about six months I began to feel the stress – of coping with clinical duties as well as administrative – becoming excessive, so I was pleased to hand over my acting command to a new Commanding Officer. The new CO and I became very good friends. It soon became evident that he was a very experienced and efficient administrative officer. After he took over, I commenced my aforementioned research study. I used to play golf with him at weekends when I returned home from London. One Saturday evening we met and arranged to play golf together on the following morning. However, he rang me early in the morning to say that he was unable to play with me because he had to play in a competition. As I hadn't entered the competition, I decided to play with a colleague of mine. We started to play after the competition had got underway. Much to our horror, as we commenced playing we saw an ambulance leaving the course. We subsequently found out that the ambulance contained the dead body of our dear CO. He had suddenly collapsed on the course and died. As I have already mentioned, we had become good friends, and Eileen had become a good friend of his wife. Eileen and I took it upon ourselves to break the tragic news to her. Her tragic loss deepened our friendship and we have managed to keep in touch ever since.

This time, as I was on detachment to a London hospital, I was not called upon to undertake the duties of acting Commanding Officer.

My work in the hospital at Tidworth was very interesting and varied. We dealt with many casualties, some of whom were seriously injured, from road traffic accidents. In those days seat belts had not yet been introduced, and, consequently, many of these patients suffered from severe facial and chest injuries. The local GPs often referred cases to us that required major surgery. There were many interesting cases. I remember the young serviceman who collapsed when he was running to his classroom. It was necessary to operate on him, and I found that he had a rupture of his spleen. His spleen was removed, and he subsequently made good recovery from the operation. It transpired that he had developed symptoms a few weeks previously of glandular fever, a condition which may cause the spleen to be at risk from spontaneous rupture, an event precipitated by the patient's physical exertion. Having fairly recently returned from service in a tropical climate, the winter of 1965–6, with its arctic conditions, was for me a contrasting experience, producing as it did, an influx of a very large number of servicemen with frostbite of their toes and fingers sustained when they were on an exercise. Although this was a very unpleasant and painful experience for the patients who sustained frostbite, it was a unique and interesting experience for me which I shall long remember.

Towards the end of 1968 I was informed that I had been posted back to Singapore as Command Consultant Surgeon to the Far East Land Forces, with the rank of Brigadier.

Chapter 13

Return to Singapore

In January 1969 I flew to Singapore. I arranged for Eileen and the children to follow me three months later. This was to allow Eileen time to arrange for our cottage to be let and for the children to complete their term at school. To begin with I lived in the Officers' Mess, and subsequently, when the family arrived, we moved out into a beautiful large army quarter in a residential area only a couple of miles from Singapore City. We inherited two very nice Chinese servants from the previous occupants of the house, a cook and an amah. We also had the services of a gardener. The children's education was well-provided for in the excellent schools they attended.

My work as Command Consultant had two main aspects, namely administrative and clinical. As regards administration, I had the responsibility for the staffing and equipping of the surgical units throughout the Command. On the clinical side, I was expected to give surgeon's advice and assistance, in the management of their difficult cases. Within the Command, there were six military hospitals. It was my duty to visit them from time to time. My visits to the surgical units of the hospitals were much appreciated by the surgeons because of the opportunity, they gave them of discussing their problems, clinical and administrative, with me at first hand. In turn, I must say, I sometimes learned a good deal from seeing their difficult cases, and discussing their management with them.

I also had to spend a good deal of time writing reports on the work I did, for submission to my Director at MOD at frequent intervals. In addition I had my own patients to see and treat in our hospital in Singapore.

An interesting facet to my work concerned my involvement in the activities of the local civilian surgical academic bodies. With my appointment as Lecturer in Surgery, I became a member of staff of the University of Singapore. I also became a Member of the Academy of Medicine and of the Surgical Society, of Singapore. Singapore was a Mecca for surgeons world-wide to visit, it being a stopover for them as they made their way from west to east or from east to west on their travels. They came mainly from the United Kingdom, Australian and America. During their short stay in Singapore, they gave presentations on subjects connected with their own particular specialist field in surgery. I, as one of their hosts, in return would take them around our Military Hospital.

My visits to our hospitals entailed a good deal of flying in various types of aircraft: large civilian airliners, small fixed wing military aircraft and helicopters. I suffered from a fear of heights which affected me when I was flying in small aircraft including helicopters. On one occasion – which was my most horrifying experience – I was travelling from Kathmandu down to Dharan in a small aircraft when the pilot decided to give me a close look at Mount Everest. In doing so, he banked the aircraft many times. Little did he know how petrified I was and how much I was suffering. On another occasion I was transported in a Meteor jet RAF fighter plane to see a very ill patient suffering from a head injury in a hospital in north Malaya. Before we took off, the pilot enquired if I had any problems about flying. I muttered something about my fear of heights. He immediately assured me that as we would be travelling so fast, and at such a height, I would not be affected by my fears. At the same time, he warned me not to press the button that was located near my seat, because, if I did, I would be ejected from the aircraft and would no longer have any fears of heights. Needless to say, this instruction instilled in my mind another fear. To add to my misery he insisted, during our journey, on swooping to a low altitude to give me a sight of the old hospitals I worked in during my National Service. Finally, as we were approaching our destination we entered a tropical storm. Subsequently, when we made our descent to land on a runway, the pilot became busy cleaning the inside of the windscreen with a rag, which surprised me, in view of all the technology that had been incorporated in the aircraft. However, in due course we made a good landing. I was grateful to the pilot for getting me to my destination so quickly and safely. Regrettably, my patient had suffered severe brain damage and died soon after I performed an exploratory operation.

I had an interesting experience during my visit to our military hospital in Penang. I had heard that the Penang Hospital had a laboratory where the venom from sea snakes was extracted, and then forwarded to Australia. In Australia it was injected into horses for the production of an anti-snake venom serum. I should mention that sea snakes were very prevalent in the waters of the Far East, and their bite was very often lethal. I decided to visit the laboratory. When I arrived, I found a technician in the process of obtaining some venom. He was holding the snake's head over the edge of a saucer which was used to collect the venom. I observed the technician had two fingers missing from his right hand. He told me that on one occasion he was disturbed by the telephone ringing and as a result, loosened his hold on the snake and was bitten by it. He immediately applied a tourniquet to the finger. Subsequently it was decided it would be safer to amputate the digit than to risk the consequences of removing the tourniquet. I have forgotten how he sustained a snake bite on the other finger.

The two highlights of my tour of duty were my participation in a jungle warfare exercise and my visit to Vietnam.

The jungle warfare exercise – in which Commonwealth forces were involved – was the largest exercise held outside Europe. Its preparation, from the point of view of the medical services, required a great deal of planning in advance and particularly logistical planning. My participation

Jungle exercise – my tent.

concerned the provision of surgical care for the casualties that might arise from it. The exercise took place in the jungles of north-east Malaya. I attached a Field Surgical Team, with myself as surgeon, to the Main Dressing Station of a Field Ambulance. In addition, if required, I had the backup of a surgical team on board an aircraft carrier anchored off the coast. However, very few casualties presented and I spent most of my time observing what was going on around me.

A good deal of my attention was drawn to the activities of the batman/ driver of the Commanding Officer of the Field Ambulance. Watching his goings-on, gave me the impression he was a 'Mr Fix It' character. At night, having no light in my tent, I was unable to read or write. The main source of electricity was the dynamo supplying the operating theatre. One evening, I found that the batman had provided me with electric lighting in my tent by running a cable off the dynamo. When I went to see him about this, I found him reclining on a comfortable armchair reading a book with a light from a lampstand beside his chair. When I thanked him for what he had done for me, he enquired if there were any other comforts, such as

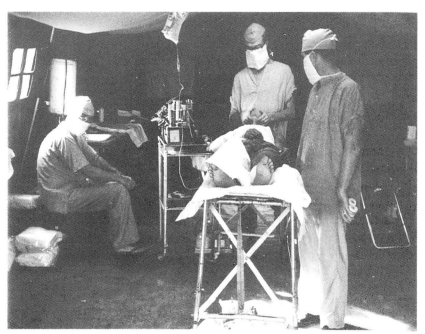

Jungle exercise – the operating theatre.

having my meals brought to me, that he could provide. I declined his offer, suspecting that he had an ulterior motive for what he had done for me already. I was one of the few officers who had permission to leave the camp and visit the local town. I also had a jeep at my disposal. One evening as I was about to drive into the town to visit the hospital there, he suddenly appeared and offered his services as my driver. After what he had done for me, I felt I couldn't refuse his offer. I must mention that I refused all his other offers, including my meals being brought to me. I continued to queue up like everybody else outside the unit kitchen for my meals. There was a story going around the unit that, as he drove with the CO at the head of the unit's column of vehicles from Singapore to the unit's location in the jungle, he allowed the unit to take a wrong turning, and then, to ingratiate himself with the CO guided it back on its right course. Incidentally, he told me that he had arranged to travel back to the UK at the end of the exercise on board the aircraft carrier. Goodness knows how he managed to make that arrangement!

One of my tasks on the exercise was to liaise with the surgeon on board the aircraft carrier. I flew out to the ship by helicopter. As we crossed the coast, the pilot mentioned that he was descending to a very low altitude in order that he could take pictures of the very beautiful coastline. I was sitting alongside the pilot with the door on my side of the helicopter wide open. In order to take his pictures, he banked the machine and leant across me. I had forgotten to tighten my safety belt, which was around my waist only. For a few moments I was looking straight down to the ground and felt my emotion of fear of heights overwhelming me. However, fortunately, I soon overcame my emotion, and from that day onwards, I have found that my fear of heights has been conquered!

When I was withdrawing my Field Surgical Team after the conclusion of the exercise, the last I saw of the Field Ambulance was it being prepared to go underground! The CO had arranged for a very wide and deep trench to be dug. He was keen to engage in a brief exercise of his own, namely to assess how his unit would function underground and camouflaged from the air. I never found out if there were any survivors from this exercise! I was pleased to have withdrawn my unit before the exercise got underway.

My Vietnam Experience

The American Army authorities allowed only a small number of British Army Officers to visit Vietnam as observers. I was fortunate in getting to know the Officer on the staff of GHQ Singapore who liaised with the Americans for the visits of our officers. In early 1971 an officer, who was due to undertake a visit, became ill. Knowing how keen I was to visit Vietnam and, my experience in counter-insurgency campaigns, he very kindly nominated me to take the place of the officer who was unable to go.

I flew to Saigon where I was met at the airport by the British Military Attaché who was to be my sponsor during my visit. To begin with, I spent some time at the Medical Command Headquarters, where I was briefed on the work of the US Army Medical Services in Vietnam. The war in Vietnam was in the nature of a counter-insurgency operation, which entailed the modification of the usual concepts of the medical services in a combat zone. There were no fronts in the tradition of World War II. In contrast to other wars, the Field Hospitals did not follow an advancing army in support of a tactical operation. They were fixed installations, and their degree of sophistication of medical equipment, specialist staff and other facilities, was far better than was available in any war previously. In fact, they provided medical care of a standard given to the citizens by a hospital in a major city in the western world. The evacuation of casualties from the field was by helicopter to the hospitals direct, with ongoing care being provided during their transportation. There were thirteen hospitals, a hospital ship and a convalescent hospital.

The helicopter evacuation system worked effectively because it was compatible with the characteristics of warfare in that country and because, of course, the Americans had air superiority. The evacuation of a casualty from the field was controlled by a central unit, which monitored the 'pick up' of the casualty, and specified the hospital he should be taken to (the central unit would know where the nearest hospital was and indeed it would know which hospital had the specialist facilities which the casualty was most in need of). The request for casualty evacuation from the field was by direct radio communication with an air ambulance helicopter unit. In the previous nine years of the war, a total of 750,000 casualties had been evacuated. There were six air ambulance medical units. When a unit received a call for the evacuation of a casualty, the helicopter crew were alerted by a siren, much like the Battle of Britain pilots were mustered during World War II. They were airborne within three minutes of receiving the call. Approximately thirty minutes later, the helicopter would be arriving at a hospital with its casualties.

After my briefing, I flew by helicopter to the US Army Field HQ at Long Binh, north of Saigon. It was located in a large clearing in the jungle. In the evening, I had dinner in the Officers' Mess. I was surprised when I entered the Mess. From the outside it had the appearance of a very large bamboo hut, but, inside, the dining room was very much up to the standard of the Dorchester Hotel in London, with wall-to-wall carpets and silver candlesticks on the dining table. To me, it all looked somewhat bizarre as I watched the officers enter the dining room wearing their tropical combat uniform and looking as if they had just returned from a patrol in the jungle. I was, incidentally, pleased to be introduced to the Commanding General of the US Army in Vietnam, who was seated at the head of the dining table.

I subsequently visited a Field Hospital which was in the vicinity of the army HQ. During my visit to this hospital, I was accommodated in a very large and sumptuous caravan. It had been imported from Texas. The hospital was the prototype of all the army hospitals built in Vietnam. It was built on a rectangular plot with huts made of tin with an inner lining of wood-fibre panels. The huts were sited in parallel lines on the long sides of the rectangle. Facilities for the immediate care of the casualty (i.e., resuscitation, operating theatres, intensive care unit, etc.) were sited

Caravan site – officers living quarters in Vietnam.

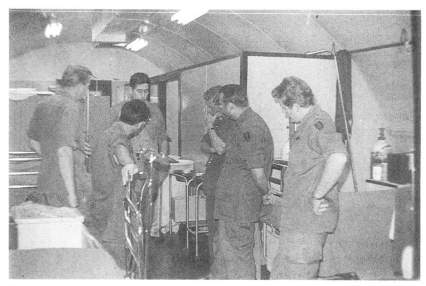

Ward Round in Field Hospital in Vietnam.

on one side of the quadrangle and the wards were on the other side. The front end of the enclosure was occupied by the Emergency Admission ward and the Administrative offices. At the rear end was the mess hall and medical supply unit. A helicopter landing pad was sited adjacent to one corner of the front of the hospital complex but sufficiently far away to protect the hospital from dust and noise. The hospital had 250 beds. An average of 1,000 patients were admitted and 700 operations were performed per month. It was staffed with thirty medical officers, including six general surgeons and various other specialists, e.g., neurosurgeons, urologists, etc. The operating theatre had six operating bays. The standard and principles of War Surgery were basically similar to our own. The equipment available for the acute care of the casualty was similar to what would be available in any modern hospital in our western civilisation.

The casualty was brought directly from the helipad to the emergency ward. He did not leave an air-conditioned environmentally controlled atmosphere throughout his acute care. He could pass quickly from the emergency ward via X-ray and laboratory facilities areas into the pre-operative ward and on to the operating theatre with least possible delay. From the operating theatre he was removed to the post operative recovery/

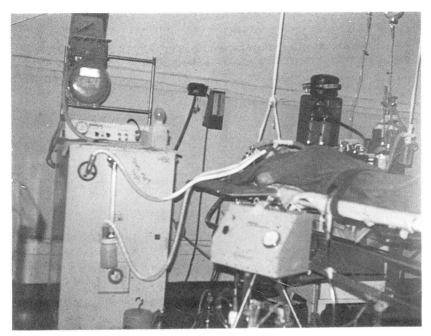

Equipment in Field Hospital in Vietnam.

intensive care unit and subsequently to the intermediate and minimal care wards.

I was very impressed with the vigorous ambulatory therapy given to the casualties, and the only seriously ill patients not to be seen out of bed on the day after an operation were those on respirators.

During my short stay in the hospital, I observed the management of a wide variety of gunshot-wound casualties, including head, neck, chest, abdominal with bowel and bladder involvement, and spine cases. I was very kindly invited to be a member of one of the teams of surgeons who were performing the operations. The drug addiction problem, which was affecting US Army personnel in Vietnam, was brought to my attention by the surgeon I was assisting at an operation when he remarked that a young casualty's loaded colon was a common finding, and that it was evidence of constipation resulting from the use of heroin, which he said was readily available and sold on the streets of Saigon at a dollar an ounce by enemy agents. Post operatively analgesia with morphia was a convenient method of treating withdrawal symptoms.

The wounds the casualties sustained were mainly from small-arms fire, and booby traps and mines, the greater proportion being from the latter. The small-arms weapons used were M16/AK47s which caused severe tissue damage and often multiple wounds. On the other hand, the mines and booby traps, because of the proximity of the casualty to the blast they created, caused severe tissue destruction with tremendous amounts of debris, dirt and secondary missiles being hurled into the wounds.

During my stay at Long Binh, I also visited an Air Ambulance Helicopter unit, and saw at first hand how the helicopter evacuation system functioned. The helicopters used were designed in a way that allowed for three-patient stretchers to be placed transversely in a tier across the fuselage and this made it relatively easy to load the casualty on the machine and to subsequently unload him. The crew consisted of a pilot, co-pilot, a crew chief who was armed and ready to defend the aircraft against enemy attack, and a medic (nursing orderly). The equipment it carried ensured that resuscitation of the casualty was ongoing during the flight to the hospital. It was escorted by a gunship, i.e., a helicopter armed with heavy

Air Ambulance Helicopter – Vietnam.

weapons, when necessary, e.g., when the pick-up point was insecure from enemy attack. Helicopter casualty evacuation was carried out at night as well as during the day. When no landing zone was available, e.g., in the jungle, a procedure known as a Hoist Operation was carried out. The hoist consisted of a winch and a cable at the end of which a forest penetrator was attached. The penetrator was shaped like a joint arrowhead and had three narrow paddle seats folded against its sides and as it plummeted downwards it penetrated the jungle roof, splintering branches and skidding off tree trunks. Usually however, a medic descended on the penetrator straddling one of the pulled-down paddles. The medic would then seat the casualty on one of the paddles and strap him to the penetrator.

Before leaving Long Behn I had lunch with the Commander of the US Army Medical Services. It was followed by an exchange of gifts, mine being a replica of our British Military Hospital, Singapore Plaque. I then flew by helicopter to Binh Thuy which was situated in the Mekong Delta, where I visited another Field Hospital. It was a much smaller hospital but nevertheless a quite busy one. About 300 patients were admitted monthly, 50 per cent of which were war casualties. It had a convalescent wing which was run by the Vietnamese for amputees. During my short stay in this hospital, I assisted at one particularly difficult operation, a repair of an injury to the main artery and vein behind the knee from a G.S.W. which had resulted in the establishment of a fistula, i.e., an abnormal communication between the two vessels. I was very impressed with the expertise of the specialist who performed the operation so successfully. My final visit was to a Vietnamese Armed Forces hospital which was located not far from the American Field Hospital. This was a most interesting experience. It was a 600-bedded hospital and had a daily admission rate of about forty surgical cases, most of whom were war casualties. High standards of management of the patients were being maintained by the surgeons in spite of an apparent shortage of nursing staff. Although it was an extremely busy hospital, and full to capacity, it appeared to be well-run and organised.

Before returning to Saigon, a helicopter pilot, with whom I had had a long discussion concerning the use of helicopters in casualty evacuation, much to my surprise, invited me to accompany him in his aircraft, when very shortly, he was to take part in the incursion into Cambodia, an action that was being taken to prevent the Viet Cong infiltrating into South Vietnam from Cambodia. Regrettably, I had to decline his invitation on the grounds that such an event was not on the official schedule of my visit to Vietnam.

Whilst waiting in Saigon to return to Singapore, I had some time to reflect on my visit to Vietnam. Most of all, I was profoundly impressed with the efficiency of the American Army Medical Services, and in particular their system of evacuating the casualty from the field to a hospital by helicopter, the management of the casualty after his arrival in the hospital and not least the dedication and expertise of the helicopter crews, surgeons and nurses. On the other hand, I found the low morale of the conscript servicemen somewhat disturbing to say the least. The conscript felt that he was fighting a war that was not being won. More importantly, he either did not understand the reasons for the war being fought or indeed was not interested in them. However the professional soldier, or 'regular' (as we refer to him in our Army) felt he had a job to do, namely the defeat of the enemy regardless of the reasons for fighting the war, and the sooner this objective was achieved, the sooner he would be back home in the USA. These professionals were indeed dedicated servicemen and I would be happy to serve with them in any conflict.

I did not see much of Saigon, but the little I did see of it, left me with two contrasting and lasting impressions. In the streets there were numerous seedy bars and cafés with Vietnamese standing outside them selling their nefarious wares. In contrast, there were some remaining French Colonial tree-lined boulevards, untouched by the ravages of war. Again, in contrast to the aspect of Saigon aforementioned, was the fascinating sight of masses of men, women and children, all beautifully dressed in clean white shirts or blouses, making their way on the streets on bicycles or Honda motor scooters.

Before departing to Singapore, it was my duty to thank the British Military Attaché for all the arrangements he had made to make my visit so pleasant and interesting, and for being so kind to me. Incidentally, when I was leaving Saigon, and was passing through immigration at the airport, an incident occurred, which made me believe that we were not very popular with Vietnamese, presumably, because, we weren't giving them the active support the Americans and the Australians were giving them. In spite of the presence of an official from the British Embassy, the immigration officials delayed my departure for some time, alleging there was some irregularity in my passport. The latter irregularity, I presumed, was to do with the fact that on entry, my passport had not been properly stamped by the immigration officials.

As I flew back to Singapore my mind was still boggled by the experience of always travelling by helicopter during my stay in Vietnam and the sight of so many of these machines at flight departure sites, lined up and ready to take off, just like taxis in a rank outside a mainline London railway station!

Farewell to Singapore

When I returned to Singapore I found life very humdrum after my Vietnam experience. The base was in the process of running down rapidly. I had time on my hands to complete a memorandum I had been writing. It was an Army Medical Directorate research study on the effects of the Vagotomy operation on the serviceman's state of fitness. However, my work in the hospital was not all humdrum. One morning, when I was scrubbing up before performing an operation on a patient's stomach, the patient collapsed during the commencement of the anaesthetic. The patient very soon developed the appearance of the 'Michelin Man' as seen in adverts for a well-known brand of car tyres. As a result of some fault in the valve in the system delivering oxygen from its cylinder, oxygen had entered her lungs under great pressure, causing rupture of the organs

Helicopter 'Taxi' rank in Vietnam.

and consequent widespread distension of her tissues with the gas. Her heart had stopped beating but fortunately, however, we very quickly identified the cause of her collapse. I immediately opened her chest and performed open heart massage and inserted drainage tubes in both sides of her chest.

These resuscitative measures had a successful outcome, and in due course we were able to proceed with her operation. She recovered extremely well from her operation, which we attributed to some extent to the hyperoxygenation her tissues had received and which enhanced the healing of her wounds. Sometime later when I reviewed her progress in my out-patient clinic, and she had had time to think about what had happened during her operation, I expected her to ask many questions and to complain about her treatment. Instead she expressed her delight with the progress she had made since she had left hospital. I hasten to add that I concealed nothing from her about what happened during the induction of her anaesthetic.

Golf course in Singapore.

One of the quite depressing features of the preparations we were making to leave, concerned the disposal of the servicemen's family pets. In anticipation that there would be no one to look after them when we left, these cats and dogs had to be taken to an Army Veterinary unit for humane disposal. On a lighter note, I have to mention a humorous but somewhat embarrassing incident that occurred when I took part in one of my last golf competitions on the island. Our British Forces Commander – a keen golfer himself – as a momento, decided to take photos of his officers as they drove off from the first tee. Much to my horror, when it came to my turn to drive off and his camera clicked, I had a 'Mulligan'! I missed the ball completely.

Another incident occurred playing golf, which caused a friend and colleague, my anaesthetist, great embarrassment. During this present tour in Singapore, we played regularly together, and as time went on, I could never understand how, when he hit his ball into the jungle, he would always manage to come back on the fairway with his next shot. During our last game before we returned to the UK, I followed him into the

Our Chinese amah holding our cat.

jungle. There I saw, as Captain Boyle might say, something no mortal man should see, my opponent's caddie preparing a good lie for my friend to play his next shot from.

Our saddest moments came when we had to say goodbye to our two Chinese servants, who had looked after us so very well and had been so kind to us.

On the 1st of August 1971, I stood outside our beloved Military Hospital, and having looked back at it for the last time, assisted in closing its gates. As I walked away, I felt that another chapter in my life had been closed, but that, however, the fond memories of my work in the hospital would always remain with me.

I had one final duty to perform before we left, and that was to say goodbye to the medical students of the University of Singapore. During my tour of duty I regularly gave lectures to them and undertook teaching ward rounds for them; I got to know them almost individually, and become very fond of them and they of me. They were mainly Chinese, but some were Indians and Malays. As a farewell gesture, they invited Eileen and me to a dinner. I sincerely hope they all have done well in their practice of medicine.

Chapter 14

Home Service Resumed

When we returned to the UK we went back to our cottage in Hampshire. My request to return to the hospital I had worked in before going to Singapore had been granted. The person who rented our cottage whilst we were away had vacated it a few days before we arrived back. He was, however, very much in arrears with his rent. He also had not paid his electricity and telephone bills. Inside the cottage there was damage to furniture and to the property generally, and outside there was damage to the lawns and flower beds. He had been using the lawns for parking cars. On top of all that, there was no trace of his whereabouts. His wife called one day looking for him. He had left her and had ceased to pay her any maintenance. When we were letting the property to him, we received a character reference from his bank manager stating that he was financially sound and that he was an engineer by profession! It now transpired that in fact he was a second-hand car salesman, and hence, the use of the lawns for parking cars. In the end, my solicitor advised me that financially, I could be worse off with the expenses of locating him and taking him to court for the non-payment of his rent and other debts.

I am pleased to say that our children did well in the schools they attended in Singapore. Our eldest son, Terence, became Head Boy of his school, a school with a thousand pupils. They settled down very well again in the local schools.

The hospital was quite busy. In addition to its care of the serviceman and his family, it had become well-established in providing treatment for patients in the local civilian population.

Not long after I returned to the UK, I woke up one morning with a very stiff neck and various other symptoms. I had difficulty in driving my car to the hospital, and when I got there, I was admitted to hospital under the

99

care of the physicians. They became very worried about me and instigated a wide variety of investigations, including a lumbar puncture, the thought of which made me wonder if they were casting too wide a diagnostic net. I thought hard about the diagnosis, and the upshot was that I remembered an injury to my neck I had sustained playing rugby many years previously. I was playing in the front row of the forwards alongside a hooker who was quite small, and as a result, succeeded in bending my neck so much that I walked around with a stiff and painful neck for some days subsequently. Since then my neck never really troubled me, but now I realised it was very likely the cause of my symptoms. An X-ray examination revealed evidence of an old and severe injury of my cervical spine. I was treated with traction applied to my neck, which soon brought about complete resolution of my symptoms. However, it was natural that I should be curious about what brought on this attack so long after the injury was sustained. It then occurred to me that it must have been precipitated by bending over the operating table during an unusual long list of cases on the day before its onset.

During my previous tour of duty in the hospital, I got to know a highly successful steeplechase jockey. He was attached to a racing stable not very far from where we lived. I became acquainted with him as a result of providing follow-up treatment of the injuries he sustained from time to time with physiotherapy. Sadly to relate he now came to see me soon after he had been discharged from a hospital following treatment for a severe injury of his arm. When I examined him I found that he had a paralysis of the limb. The specialist, who had been treating him, advised him to retire from racing, because he felt that the prospects of his recovery from the paralysis were very poor, and in any case, recovery, if indeed it did occur, would take some considerable time. It appeared that he was turning to me for arbitration on the decision he had to make, i.e., to retire now, or wait and see if in due course he would make a good recovery from his injury. I agreed with the advice the specialist had given him, and accordingly, advised him not to defer his retirement. That evening, I was rung up by a friend in London. He informed me that I had been quoted in the Evening News by Reuters as having advised a famous steeplechase jockey to retire on medical grounds. The following morning, MOD requested an explanation of how I became involved in a matter that had nothing to do with my military duties. In mitigation, I pleaded that my actions in this matter could be regarded as good P.R. duties.

Some incidents in the life of our cat are worthy of mention here. We brought him to Singapore by sea to join us there. During the voyage the ship's cook took a liking to him and fed him too much. As a result, when he arrived in Singapore, he was so much overweight that he could hardly walk. He managed in Singapore to avoid being eaten by snakes and other reptiles and to survive the heat and, in due course, returned by air to the UK. After six months quarantine he rejoined us in our cottage. However, in contrast to his uneventful sojourn in the Far East, his return to his own environment was marked by a near tragedy, when he was struck by a passing car on the road outside our cottage, and later on, when we left him in a cats-and-dogs' home whilst we were on holiday, he absconded. Fortunately, somehow or other, he was found about a mile from the home on top of a tall tree.

At the end of a year in my present appointment, I was posted to our premier hospital in London, i.e., the Queen Alexandra Military Hospital, Millbank, as Consultant Surgeon and at the same time was appointed Assistant Professor of Military Surgery at our Royal Army Medical College. I was given to understand that these appointments, which were to be of six months duration, were in the nature of a course of preparation for my assumption of the role of Director of Army Surgery and Consulting Surgeon to the Army in due course. I felt that I was very fortunate. I never, during my Army career, sought higher office. I was always happy and contented working as a surgeon in whatever part of the world I happened to be in. Looking back, I found that I had set off, approximately twenty years previously, on an unknown journey into the field of Military Surgery and, in spite of my fear of heights, it now appeared that I had been climbing a ladder all the time.

The six months I spent in Millbank was probably the busiest time I had spent in the Army. My time was spent mainly in learning as much as possible, in the short time I had available, about the work my next appointment would involve, giving lectures and teaching young medical officers, and in my clinical duties in the hospital. I also had to meet and get to know the Honorary Consultants to the Army, who were renowned civilian specialists in the various fields of Surgery.

Our hospital at Millbank was our main teaching hospital. It was the centre of excellence for the treatment of the serviceman and servicewoman and his or her family. Our Honorary Consultants are always happy to see and advise on the management of any particular case in the hospital and, if necessary, treat the patient in their own specialist centre. This ensures that the best possible treatment is always available to the soldier and his family. During this time, I lived in our Officers' Mess at Millbank. One of my responsibilities as a living-in member of the Mess was to look after any senior officer from outside our Corps who was staying overnight in it. One evening, when performing these latter duties, I dropped a big clanger! I was standing up at the dining room table and was about to introduce a very senior General, who was seated alongside me, to a number of young medical officers, when I looked up at the long line of portraits of past Director Generals of our Corps hung on the wall opposite me. The portrait of a DG, who I believed qualified at my own University, caught my eye and as I commenced my introductions I gave the DG's name as the General's name! Fortunately, when I explained to the General what had happened, he laughed and took my mistake in good spirits.

On a more sombre note, one evening, after attending a clinical meeting in a London hospital, I was invited to a colleague's house for dinner and subsequently, having stayed overnight in his house, didn't realise I had breached a security regulation. Apparently, on that night there was a high security alert for possible terrorist action and it was imperative, consequently, that I should have notified the Mess of my whereabouts. The next morning I received an admonishment and rebuke from the Commandant of the College for the apprehension my absence had caused the authorities concerned.

Chapter 15

The Climax of my Military Career

I assumed the appointment of Director of Army Surgery and Consulting Surgeon to the Army in April 1973. To get off to a good start in my new appointment, I donned the uniform worn by my colleagues at MOD i.e., dark suit and bowler hat and carried an umbrella and a brief case.

My work involved me in a wide range of activities and, looking back, I can only summarise them as being mainly of an administrative, academic, and clinical nature.

Incidentally, and before I forget, I feel I must pay tribute to my predecessor, Norman Rogers. He was always very kind and helpful to me when I was a member of his team of consultants. Now that I was following in his footsteps, I felt that, because the work he undertook as Director had been so very well accomplished, I would have to strive very hard to emulate even some of his fine achievements.

On the administrative side, my responsibilities entailed planning the careers of surgeons from SHO right through to Consultant grade, the organisation and staffing and the equipping, of the surgical units in our Military hospitals, and the organisation of our Surgical Services, including the updating and scaling of equipment, etc., in the event of another war. There were fifty-five surgeons of all grades, and surgical units in thirteen military hospitals, involved in my aforementioned responsibilities.

In the academic field, my main responsibility was the planning and organisation of the training of our surgeons and, in particular, their Higher Surgical Training programmes. At the time I assumed the appointment of Director, the Royal College of Surgeons had instituted the latter Training programme for all civilian surgeons. Here I must give due credit to my predecessor, Norman Rogers, for the excellent work he had done in introducing and getting Higher Surgical Training in the Army well under-way and established. The programme involved a mandatory period of four years in posts that the Royal College had inspected and subsequently recognised as being suitable for training a surgeon for accreditation as a Consultant. In order that our surgeons, when they achieved Consultant status, would be on equal footing with their peers in civilian life, it was imperative that I organised training programmes that would be recognised by the Royal College. Thankfully, the Royal College agreed our Training schedules provided that two of the four years were spent by our surgeons in civilian-recognised hospital training posts. This, of course, meant that I had to spend a great deal of time and effort in arranging with my civilian colleagues for the provision of suitable posts for my training programmes, and also, in coping with the problems of staffing our surgical units, resulting from the absence of some surgeons on surgical training in civil-ian life.

Other aspects of my involvement in the academic field included Research and Development and, in particular, missile wound research programmes, training of our surgeons in War Surgery, First Aid Training, and the management of mass casualties. These academic activities in-volved me in attending numerous committee meetings and symposia, and attending meetings of various academic bodies, including our own Col-lege and the Royal Colleges. Without the valuable and expert assistance afforded to me by the Professor of Military Surgery, I would have found it very difficult to undertake and discharge all of these duties effectively.

There were many facets to my work in the field of clinical surgery. Apart from the duties I performed acting as Consultant Surgeon, I also acted as surgeon in charge of the Army Surgical Oncology Unit at Millbank. This unit had a very long association with the world-renowned Oncology unit at the Westminster Hospital and indeed, it could be said that it was more or less amalgamated with the latter unit. Over the years, a protocol had been established, whereby, soon after a patient had been admitted to our unit, he or she would be taken to the Joint Neoplastic Clinic at the Westminster Hospital where the necessary investigations of the patient's condition would be planned. When the results of the investi-gations were to hand, the patient would return to the clinic and, following a discussion involving the Professor of Oncology, Charles Westbury, the Consultant i/c of the Radiotherapy Unit, Dr Ken Newton, and other high-powered specialists, a schedule of the treatment the patient was to be given would be drawn up. Any surgery that was necessary would be carried out by me or by my colleague in our unit at Millbank, or indeed, by the Professor if the proposed operation was not within the range of my surgical expertise.

As I recall, cancer of the breast was the most common neoplasm that presented in our unit and the next common lesion presenting was cancer of the stomach and bowel, followed perhaps by cancer of the testis. I found my involvement in this field of medicine to be a depressing and humbling experience. The discussion I always had to have with patients who had advanced cancer and not long to live, about the probable outcome of their treatment, could be very exacting. However, I, after a great deal of thought and soul searching, soon came to believe that it was preferable to adopt an air of optimism and, as a result, allow the patient to have some freedom from worry and anxiety during the short time he or she still had to live. In this respect, I remember a young mother who was in hospital over Christmas, very ill from advanced breast cancer. She had three young children. Her husband had left her some time previously. I always gave her hope and encouragement. On Christmas Day she appeared to be quite happy and enjoyed the day in company with her children and her relatives in the ward. She died not long afterwards.

The Professor of Oncoloy, his colleague, the Consultant in Radiotherapy and indeed, every member, both medical and nursing, of the Oncology Unit were very kind and considerate to my patients and me. The attention and care given by the Unit to the serviceman and his family, when they attended it, was very special and made me feel proud to be associated with it. When, subsequently, the hospital conferred on me the appointment of Honorary Consultant to the Unit, I felt that it was one of the most important events of my whole medical career. Some years later, when there was talk of the hospital being closed down and the Unit being moved to another hospital, it gave me great pleasure to write to the press and inform the public at large of the wonderful association of the Army unit with the Westminster Hospital and what its loss would mean to the serviceman and his family.

I found the treatment of bone cancer very depressing for the reasons that this form of malignant disease usually affected young male patients and the surgery involved in their treatment could be very mutilating. On two occasions it was necessary to amputate the patients' lower limb by disarticulating it through the hip. Of all the operations I performed throughout my surgical career, the latter surgical procedures caused me the most mental stress.

The highlight of my involvement in general surgery occurred when a case of inflammation of that organ, the pancreas, once more raised its ugly head! I must hastily add that it has been my lot, over the years, to be concerned with the management of the complications of acute pancreatitis in quite a few patients, the previous fulminating case being the one I recorded during my service in Singapore, when the aggressive disease extended into the patient's chest. On this occasion, the inflammation of the organ caused the patient to suffer from a severe haemorrhage. The patient was under the care of the physicians, and when I was asked to see him, he already had had twenty-seven pints of blood. When I explored his abdomen, much to my horror, I found that his haemorrhage was arising from the Splenic artery, the artery that extents transversely across the upper margin of the organ and which now had the appearances of a large German sausage. The blood was spouting from it as if from a garden watering can! Immediate control of the bleeding was achieved by the application of pressure by my assistant to a pack that had been placed on the artery. Because of the widespread dense inflammatory reaction in the surrounding tissues, it was impossible for me to locate a healthy proximal position of the artery and ligate it. As always in situations like this one, I left the operating table and sat down on a stool and gave some thought to our predicament. I soon realised that, taking into account the military strategy that when an enemy has dug in to such an extent, one should attack him, if possible, coming down from high ground, which in this case was the chest. I duly returned to the table, and, having opened the patient's chest, located the main artery of the patient's trunk and traced it down into the abdomen, to where it gives off an axis of vessels, one of which was the Splenic artery. I had no difficulty in ligating the vessel at this site. The application of this ligature brought about immediate cessation of the bleeding. The patient, in due course, made a good recovery from the operation.

To say the least, when I was Director I led an extremely busy life. I had numerous meetings to attend. They were often held in the evenings, and at weekends. They included, as previously mentioned, attendances at committee meetings involved in the training of Surgeons, Research and Development, First Aid Training, etc., and attendances at meetings held in our Royal Army Medical College, and in the Royal College of Surgeons. I also had TA War Surgery Symposia to attend.

I also had to spend considerable time writing reports for submission to my DG and to the various departments within the Medical Directorate of MOD. In addition to those aforementioned commitments, I also had a good deal of travelling to do, visiting surgical units in our hospitals at home and overseas. Overseas, I had to pay visits to surgical units in Cyprus, Oman, Nepal, Hong Kong, Belize and Germany. My journey to

Belize was quite eventful. I flew from Brize Norton in an RAF plane carrying the British Ambassador to Washington's mail. It was in the middle of a bad winter and there was snow on the runway. In order to make conditions easy for take off, the plane carried a reduced amount of fuel. We flew to Prestwick, where the weather conditions were much better, and refuelled there. Subsequently, we stopped at Ottawa for a few hours. At Washington, our destination, I was met by a British Army Liaison Officer. He informed me that I had missed my connection, a direct flight to South America. Consequently, he had to put me on a shuttle service Delta airways plane to New Orleans. The plane had the appearance of an old two-engined Dakota. The pilot appeared to be in a great hurry to get to our destination. En route, we stopped at several cities, Richmond, Virginia, etc., and at each stop he would move the plane very quickly up to and at times almost into the terminal building in his rush to be airborne again! When I reached New Orleans, I found I was too late – it was almost midnight – to catch a flight to Belize. I stayed overnight in a hotel not far from the airport, as I had an early morning flight to catch. My next frustration presented, when I found that I had to change planes in Mexico for the final stage of my journey to Belize.

My visit to Belize resulted from the strain the secondment of our surgeons in Higher Training programmes to civilian hospitals was putting on the staffing of our surgical units and, in particular, those overseas. My mission in this instance, was to find out if the local civilian surgeon, who was well-qualified and experienced, would agree to becoming involved in the care of our servicemen stationed in Belize. Happily, he agreed. When I visited the civilian hospital, I found it to be adequately staffed and equipped. Incidentally, however, I was somewhat unhappy when I observed that the entrance to the Casualty Department was located in a street called Mortuary Lane!

Belize City is the capital of what used to be British Honduras. The British troops were stationed there as a deterrent against any hostile action by the neighbouring country, Guatemala. Belize City was built on the banks of a river and, where the river flowed into the Caribbean Sea. Somerset Maughan once described it as being the 'end of the earth'! The climate there is very hot and humid all year round. The city is quite small, undeveloped, and not very prosperous. I stayed in the only fairly high-class hotel, the King George. It was on the sea front, and from it one got beautiful views of the world's second largest barrier reef. The unpleasant aspects of the environment, however, were the high humidity and the never-ending attacks of mosquitoes and sandflies.

Mortuary Lane – Entrance to the Casualty Department of the Hospital in Belize.

My return journey was uneventful, a direct flight to the UK in an RAF VC10 aircraft.

Oman, with a desert extending on a plateau from the sea to a range of mountains faraway inland, and its dry heat and high temperature, contrasted very much with the terrain and climate of Belize. When I was in Muscat, the temperature rose to a 110 degrees!

During my visit, I met up with an Iranian Field Surgical Team. The surgeon was Professor of Surgery in Tehran. He had been called up for military service in Oman as part of Iran's contribution to the war being fought against the Yemeni insurgents. He was very pleased to meet me and have the opportunity to discuss the management of war casualties with another military surgeon. We also had a Field Surgical Team in Oman, and the purpose of my visit was to see how soon we could withdraw it, because at that time our force there was being run down. Whilst I was there I had an interesting experience. I was travelling in a jeep across a wide and deep wadi, when a sudden cloudburst occurred. Very soon, our vehicle was submerged by a torrential wave of water coming down from a hillside into the wadi. We, however, managed to escape from our vehicle

Belize City.

Me in Belize.

and climb onto the bank of the wadi. Much to our surprise, some Arabs suddenly appeared as if from nowhere and proceeded to salvage our jeep. Fortunately, we were accompanied by a radio-operator, and he very quickly sent out a call to the nearest Army unit for assistance. Upon the arrival of some Army vehicles, our Arab gentlemen retreated into the desert, from whence they had come!

My visit to Oman, involved meeting the Minister of Health. He offered to me the use of the facilities of a new hospital that had just been opened.

In return, I proffered him advice on the recruitment of nurses for the staffing of the hospital.

My return journey to the UK turned out to be eventful. When we were still some flying time from Heathrow, a stewardess asked me to see a female passenger who was quite ill. I found that she appeared to be suffering from a form of Meningitis. Subsequently, the pilot, being very anxious about her, wondered if he should make an emergency stop at Paris. I assured him it wasn't necessary, provided he arranged for a doctor and an ambulance to be on stand-by at Heathrow. In return for my medical assistance, he arranged for the stewardess to present me with a bottle of whiskey!

My visits to Belfast were symbolic from several points of view. My surgical training really got under way when I was Resident Surgical Officer in the Royal Victoria Hospital there. Now, thirty years later, I returned to the hospital to pay my respects to my mentors. Alas, I should have known that, by now most of them had retired. Since my time working in the hospital, it had gained international renown for its expertise in the management of patients injured by bullets or bombs. It had pioneered advances in the treatment of patients in the fields of both medicine and surgery. It had won the respect and admiration of both communities, and in the wards Catholics and Protestants lay side by side, being treated by doctors and nurses from both sides of the great 'divide'. I had commenced my military surgical career treating casualties from the terrorist campaign in Malaya, and now at the end of my career, I was visiting a city of the UK where our military surgeons were engaged in treating casualties resulting from a terrorist campaign there. I was also seeing what I had observed in other countries where terrorism was rife, namely, people going about their daily lives, unperturbed by the emotion of fear engendered by being at risk to the murderous acts of terrorists. I recall a long line of school children walking into their school in an orderly and well-behaved manner, whilst, nor far away, a car bomb was being exploded by the security forces.

As a member of the Committee responsible for the revision of the NATO Handbook on Emergency War Surgery, I visited NATO Headquarters in Belgium. I stayed in a small town not far from Waterloo, and as a result, availed myself of the opportunity of looking at the two square miles of ground where the battle was fought. For a few moments, I gave some thought to the terrible suffering of the wounded, remembering that after about eight hours of fighting, 40,000 dead and wounded lay on this relatively small area of ground. That morning, when I was having breakfast in my hotel, I got talking to a local inhabitant. He told me that the day was the anniversary of the Battle of Waterloo, and that on each anniversary day, the local newspaper published a reason why Napoleon lost the Battle. This year, he said, the reason given was that one of Napoleon's Field Marshals was an addict to strawberries and ice-cream. On the morning of the Battle, he was sitting in an inn eating the aforementioned, and when told that Wellington's army was on the move, he had some more helpings of strawberries and ice-cream before he left to join his troops, and as a result, he arrived late on the battlefield. Subsequently, his flank of Napoleon's Army was overrun, and the battle was lost!

Before I returned home, I also took the opportunity of visiting the battlefields of Mons where the Great War began and ended, and Somme where the casualties amounted to 800,000. It brought to my mind the courage and self-sacrifice of the RAMC, including its nurses and its stretcher-bearers, during that War, and during which, the Corps won seven VCs, and two bars.

Incidentally, during my overseas tours I visited seven countries and ten of our surgical units.

In this discourse on my travels, I feel I must mention an incident which caused me a great deal of embarrassment. It occurred when I was visiting Berlin. When I landed at the Templehof International airport in Berlin, a staff car drove onto the runway to collect me. As I placed my luggage in the boot of the car, I put my brief case on the ground behind me. Subsequently, when I arrived at the Officers' Mess I was to stay in, I received a phone call from the Military Police informing me that a brief case lying on the airport runway, which they now presumed was mine, had caused a security alert, which resulted in the airport being closed down for a brief period!

One of the oddities about visiting Berlin concerned the fact that one was allowed to visit East Berlin. I used to pass through 'Checkpoint Charlie' in full uniform in a staff car. One could do a lot of sightseeing as many of the historical buildings of pre-war interest were in the East sector of Berlin. We were allowed to enter stores and purchase goods if we wanted to. Many of the items sold in the shops were cheaper than they were in West Berlin. I felt most uncomfortable when I entered a large store, because of being stared at continuously and particularly by young people. I was always pleased to return to West Berlin and get away from the air of gloom and depression that seemed to pervade the whole environment of East Berlin.

In April 1974, I was promoted to the rank of Major General. In the final years of my military career, honours were conferred upon me, which I feel resulted from the splendid work the surgeons of our Corps accomplished, and indeed honoured them just as much as they honoured me. I was very honoured by my peers in the Royal College of Surgeons of England when they graciously admitted me to their Fellowship *ad eundem*. The very highlight of my surgical career must have been my appointment as Honorary Surgeon to the Queen. This appointment entailed my attendance at Buckingham Palace, during a Garden Party or a Royal Banquet and at Investitures. I am very pleased to say that I was very honoured when, on the occasion I performed my last duty before I retired, I was granted a private audience with Her Majesty. Finally, at the climax of my military career, I was awarded the CB.

In closing this story of my career as a surgeon in the RAMC, I reflect upon what have been my main experiences. I travelled a great deal and visited many countries from here to Hong Kong and indeed, as far as South America. In my work as a surgeon, I observed the ravages inflicted on man by his fellowman, man's inhumanity to man, in the name of so-called justice and liberty, in the streets of Belfast, the jungles of Malaya, Borneo and Vietnam and the towns and villages of Cyprus.

On the other hand, I was privileged in seeing some of the wonders of nature, a great barrier reef, the jungles of Malaya, Borneo, and Vietnam, the wide dusty horizons of Oman, the beauty of the Indian continent, and the splendour of Mount Everest.

I was privileged to have served in Singapore for so long, because of its orderliness, cleanliness and its freedom from petty crime, vandalism, and hooliganism. In addition, I admired the students who attended my lectures at the University for being so attentive, appreciative, decorous and well-mannered.

Altogether, I worked in twelve Military Hospitals. They were all exceedingly well run, staffed and equipped. The Medical Officers and QA Nursing Officers were always dedicated and devoted to the care of their patients.

I shall always remember the unfailing devotion to duty of the other rank male and female nurses, and the hardworking and efficient technicians, who worked in the operating theatre and in the various other departments, Radiological, Pathological, etc., and who were always cheerful and co-operative no matter how great their workload was.

Finally, my own work as a surgeon was always very challenging and interesting and particularly rewarding in the last years of my career when I was involved in the care of Oncology patients. I was also, in these latter years, gratified to see our surgeons' Higher Surgical Training programme come to fruition, and as a result, our Consultants were now on an equal footing with their peers in civilian life.

Sadly, soon after I retired, one of my brothers who was a GP in London, collapsed suddenly and died. A few weeks later my mother died.

Chapter 16

Return to Civilian Life

I retired from the Army in April 1978. Before I retired, I was fortunate in gaining an appointment in the NHS as a Consultant in Accident and Emergency Medicine. I was due to take up the appointment in July.

Meanwhile, I worked for two weeks as a locum tenens for a surgeon in Holland. The hospital I worked in was situated in a small but beautiful town about thirty miles north-east of Amsterdam. My work entailed running a Casualty Department and being responsible for the treatment of all the acute surgical cases admitted to the hospital. I enjoyed my short stay in Holland very much. The hospital staff were very kind to me and looked after me well. The hospital was not busy, and I really had only two serious cases to deal with. One was a German tourist who sustained chest injuries in a road-traffic accident. He recovered well from his injuries, after the implementation of chest tube drainage. The other case, a young girl, was admitted on my last day on duty with acute abdominal pain and vomiting. At an exploratory operation, I found that she had a congenital pouch (diverticulum), arising from her small bowel, which had undergone torsion and, as a result, had become gangrenous. I removed the part of the bowel the diverticulum was arising from. When I returned to the UK, I spent an anxious time waiting to hear from the surgeon I had handed her case over to, about how she had progressed after her operation. In due course, when I heard from him, I was very relieved to know that she had recovered well from her operation and had progressed well subsequently.

My appointment in the NHS was in an old hospital in Ealing, West London, which was to be closed and replaced by a new hospital. The newly built hospital was due to open in March 1979. Meanwhile, whilst I was working in the existing hospital, I was instructed to undertake the planning and organisation of the A&E department in the new hospital. To

115

carry out the work involved in the latter project, I applied for, and was granted, a period of absence from duty in order that I could visit other hospitals throughout England, and learn from the experiences of consultants in them and from the way they ran their departments. Altogether, I visited thirteen hospitals. I learned a great deal. The consultants were very kind to me and invariably went to a great deal of trouble demonstrating the running of their departments to me, and briefing me on the problems they encountered. From this experience, I realised there were numerous factors involved in the efficient running of an A&E department. However, looking back at casualty evacuation from the battlefield, I felt that there were some principles involved in that procedure that had some essence in their application, believe it or not, to the running of a peacetime casualty department. They were, namely, good means of communication, and an efficient method for the flow of patients within the department and through the department to other departments and the hospital wards. I was fortunate in that the Administrator of the hospital was a keen, energetic, and highly efficient young man. He had many of the attributes of a good Army Administration Officer. He gave me his utmost co-operation. He had installed in the department for me the most up-to-date modern intercom system. It provided instant communication between the Consultant and his staff at various locations throughout the Department, and also allowed any member of the staff to call for assistance in any part of the unit. In addition, there was a hot line for incoming calls from the Ambulance service, alerting the department of the impending arrival of serious accident or emergency cases. For the patients 'flow system', I used different coloured tapes positioned on the floor of the department. The tapes were made of material that would withstand wear and tear indefinitely. Each coloured tape represented the way to a particular part of the department, or to other departments elsewhere or to hospital wards.

I had an excellent staff of doctors and nurses, and indeed of reception clerical staff. The Sister in charge and her staff were all very dedicated and conscientious, and worked exceedingly well as a team. My medical officer staff consisted of eight, mostly young, doctors. Some of them were from overseas. I was pleased with the way they performed their duties, and cannot recall them causing me to have to deal with any serious problems they created. There were also two GPs working part-time in the department. They had worked in the old hospital for some years. They were very loyal to me and gave me great support in the running of the department. The department was very busy and, in the first year of its existence, dealt with 30,000 patients. It was very well-equipped. It had a well-organised resuscitation room, and, a twelve-bedded ward, for the recovery of patients from general anaesthesia, short-term observation of patients, and overnight stay of cases. Special clinics, namely, follow-up and paediatric, were held within the department. As a good liaison exercise, I gave regular lectures to the local Ambulance personnel, which gave me the opportunity to meet them and get to know them.

Not long after the opening of the new hospital, it became apparent to me that a good deal of my staff's time was being taken up dealing with patients suffering from minor ailments that should have been dealt with by their own G.P.s. I must hasten to add that this situation developed through no fault of the G.P.s. In resolving the problem, I had recourse to look back to my medical student days, when the Casualty Officer, in the Department I worked in, resorted to very unusual and drastic measures (recorded in an earlier chapter) to deal with the casualty overload that confronted him daily. However, I felt that there must be a more refined solution to the problem. I called a meeting of the local G.P.s, and discussed the situation with them. As a result, some reduction in the number of attendances of these aforementioned patients occurred, but regrettably, as time went on, we were still left with a significant number attending. Finally, in the end, I felt I must give consideration to establishing a G.P.s Surgery within the Department, as it appeared to be the only way of resolving the problem!

In addition to running my own A&E department, I also worked on a part-time basis as Consultant to another department in a famous teaching hospital, the Hammersmith Hospital. My work there was mainly in the academic field, teaching the staff in the department and taking part in tutorials for the young doctors and medical students attending the hospital.

The highlight of my work occurred when the hospital became involved in the treatment of casualties from the riots in Southall in April 1979. Altogether we received a total of forty-seven casualties. The arrangements to deal with the casualties did not invoke our major accident procedure and, instead, were based on the use of the Department as a casualty clearing station. The large treatment area was taken over for the reception and sorting of the casualties. The casualties were initially sorted out into major and minor cases. The minor cases were quickly cleared from the reception area and sent to an adjacent part of the Department, which was normally used for patients requiring treatment of minor injuries, e.g., suturing of wounds. The major cases were classified according to a system of priority for resuscitation and treatment, including surgery. There was one priority one case, a head injury that required immediate surgery for extradural haemorrhage. Incidentally, the commonest injury, both major and minor, resulted from trauma to the head. The main problem encountered in the treatment of the casualties, was excluding the possibility of internal injuries or major head injury in patients who arrived in the department somewhat frightened, confused and dazed. It is known that people who are in the vicinity of a disaster situation may become afflicted by a sense of terror, and be unable to speak or decide what to do. A similar sense of terror must have been engendered in people at the Southall riots. Lord Moran in *The Anatomy of Courage* distinguished between two states of fear in war; so-called shell-shock, which he designated as 'commotional shock', and 'emotional shock' in which a man is frightened by only his thoughts. Most of the casualties from the Southall riots suffering from minor injuries, when first examined, could perhaps be described as being in a state of commotional shock. On the other hand, some attendants, ambulance and police, arriving with casualties seemed to be afflicted by emotional shock, and for example, were over anxious about their casualties. Incidentally, psychiatrists treating American servicemen who had served in the Vietnam War, reported that many of them who had suffered from a form of emotional shock, later developed symptoms of the 'Post Traumatic Stress Syndrome'.

In the performance of my administrative duties, I had many contentious problems to deal with, two of which I feel I should mention. During the Southall riots, I had the police and the media to contend with in preserving the strict confidentiality of the information contained in patients' medical documents. The other arose when a night porter refused to undertake an urgent and vital task in the department on the grounds that he had just finished his night shift and was about to go off duty. The following morning, I found him being interviewed by a hospital administrative officer in the presence of a trade union official. I am not quite sure what the outcome of the interview was. However, at the end of it, I informed the officials, that, since the porter was a member of my staff, it was my responsibility to decide on how he should be disciplined. I then took him to my office and interviewed him. I pointed out to him that he was a very important member of my Casualty Department team, and as such, he must in future put the care of our patients above all other considerations, including working to a fixed-time schedule. Admonishing him in that way, rather than disciplining him, resulted in him becoming a highly dedicated and conscientious porter.

Another aspect of the work of the department was its possible involvement in the management of what I called 'tropical diseases on the banks of the River Thames'. The hospital was on the route into London from Heathrow, taken by immigrants and other travellers arriving from overseas. It was always conceivable that these air travellers, if they became ill shortly before they commenced their journey or during their flight, might seek treatment in a hospital on their way into London from the airport. The diseases they might suffer from were many and varied. When they presented in the form of a fever, then, perhaps the most common one was Malaria. On the other hand, at that time Lassa Fever was considered to be the most dangerous from the point of view of its being highly contagious and frequently fatal. Although only a few cases had been reported in the UK, it was highly endemic in West Africa. It was vital that these cases were diagnosed early and rapidly isolated. Consequently, arrangements had to be made in the department for the isolation of any case of a fever of unknown origin presenting in a patient during the three weeks of his or her arrival from West Africa.

My work in the hospital kept me very busy, and at times I had to be on duty for very long hours. I was pleased to find that our Administrator was a very keen and indeed proficient golfer. He and I managed to play some enjoyable rounds of golf together during the summer evenings. I also had the interesting experience of acting as the official medical officer in attendance at a Test match at the Oval, when one of our Orthopaedic surgeons, who was the official medical officer, asked me to stand in for him. England were playing India. I had the pleasure of having lunch with celebrated media cricket commentators. However, the cricket was not very exciting, as it was the final day of the match, and England appeared to be winning it quite comfortably. My involvement as medical officer was also not very exciting, as the only casualty that presented throughout the day was a young boy who trod on a nail!

After I had been working as a Consultant in A&E medicine for about fifteen months, I found the mental and physical stress, of not having a Senior Registrar to deputise for me and to share some of the workload with me, becoming excessive. I felt that I had now accomplished my original objective which was to assist the local Health District in establishing the A&E Department in their new hospital.

I waited long enough before leaving, for my successor to get to know all about the work and the running of the department, and indeed worked with him for a short time after he was appointed, as an unpaid Honorary Consultant on a part-time basis.

At my farewell party, an incident occurred that both gratified and humbled me. During the party a porter walked up to me and presented me with a gift of a pipe on behalf of all the portering staff. Receiving a present from a porter, the most junior member of my staff, was one of the most memorable experiences of my entire medical career.

Finally, before closing this chapter on my experience of working as a Consultant in the NHS, albeit for only a brief period, I feel that I ought to mention that as a result of this experience I came to the conclusion that NHS hospitals would be better run and organised, if a sufficient number of the consultants in each hospital were employed on a full-time basis, and as a result be involved in the running of the hospital to a greater extent than they are when employed on a part-time basis.

A facet of my return to civilian life was being aware that, being a doctor, one could at any time day or night have to render assistance in a sudden medical emergency situation. The first occasion I became involved in such a situation was when I was driving down a busy street, and saw a young lady lying on the pavement in the throes of an epileptic fit. I drove my car onto the pavement to near where she lay. I found that the spasm of her fit had caused her to bite her tongue. However, as one expected, she soon came out of the tonicphase of her fit, and her jaw relaxed releasing her tongue. Incidentally, a passing motorist threw a pencil to me, presumably, thinking I needed the use of a gag! Subsequently, when she recovered from her fit, I took her to a doctor's surgery which was nearby.

On another occasion, I found a motor cyclist sitting in the middle of a road propped up against the side of a car that he had been in collision with. The driver of the vehicle, an elderly lady, was still sitting in the car, suffering from shock. The motor cyclist, who was fully conscious, was bleeding fairly profusely from a neck wound. A friend who was with me, had a clean handkerchief which I placed in the wound. I was then able to apply pressure to the wound, which brought about cessation of the bleeding. In the meantime somebody had rung for an ambulance. A lesson I learnt from this incident, was to make known to the police and the ambulance personnel one's professional status as soon as they arrive, because, otherwise they are apt to push you aside, an action I experienced, thinking that you may be doing more harm than good to the casualty.

An unusual experience concerned the motor cyclist who had sustained severe concussion in an accident. When I arrived on the scene, he was refusing to wait for the ambulance that had been rung for, and was about to depart in spite of the efforts of bystanders. I eventually got through to him how essential it was that he waited for the ambulance to arrive and take him to hospital.

Very early one Sunday morning, as I was driving along a deserted street in a London suburb on my way to my golf club, and accompanied by a friend of mine, I saw ahead of me a man lying on the road. Having stopped and examined him, we found he was an elderly man suffering from serious injuries no doubt sustained in a hit-and-run accident. Soon after we commenced to resuscitate him, we realised he had been dead for some time. It was not long before an ambulance arrived. A detective, who happened to be passing the scene of the accident in his car, proceeded to investigate the incident. Having taken statements from us, he allowed us to continue on our journey. Perhaps, it was fortunate that my friend was also a doctor. In such a situation, it is nice to have a colleague with you.

Finally, I was reminded how we are always at risk to the unexpected affecting our daily lives, when, one morning as I was shaving I heard a horrific noise coming from outside the front of my house. When I went to find out what had happened, I found a car upside down on the middle of the road in front of my residence. The car driver was in the process of climbing out of his upturned vehicle. My front garden wall was completely demolished. He apparently had lost control of his vehicle, and as a result struck my wall and ricochetted off it. Very soon several police cars and fire brigade vehicles arrived at the scene of the accident, and not too long afterwards, an air ambulance helicopter. This was undoubtedly an unexpected response from the emergency services to this particular road traffic accident. Apparently the person who had made the 999 phone call had given the impression that a major RTA with a pile-up of vehicles had occurred. This impression was gained from the fact that many vehicles including a bus had stopped suddenly with screeching of brakes, just short of the upturned car. Meanwhile, having examined the casualty I found that he had sustained a cut on his ear only.

Chapter 17

The Finale of my Medical Career

It so happened that at the time I was relinquishing my civilian consult-ant's appointment, a vacancy occurred in the composition of an Army Medical Board. The members were all retired senior Army Medical Offic-ers who had been specialists in a particular field of medicine. I was very fortunate in having my application to fill the vacancy accepted.

The Medical Board sat in the Queen Elizabeth Military Hospital, in South-East London. The work of the Board entailed the medical examina-tion of civilian candidates for Commissions in the Army, which meant in most cases an assessment of their fitness for entry to Sandhurst; an as-sessment of a serviceman or a servicewoman's fitness to perform his or her military duties, which in some cases meant their invaliding or dis-charge from the Army; and the medical examination of pensioners suffering from injuries or illness attributable to or aggravated by military service. A short time after my appointment I became President of the Board, and later on my duties also involved being President of the final appeal Ministry of Defence Army Medical Board.

I found the work of President of the Boards very interesting and indeed at times fascinating. It was very demanding on one's resources of clinical, administrative, and communicative skills. In the assessment of an indi-vidual's functional capacity, clear and concise thinking, and the use of sound common sense, was required. The record of the Boards Proceedings had to be regarded as an important medico-legal document, as it could be quoted from by agencies outside the Army Medical Services in the event of an appeal against its findings. The findings of the Board could have profound effects on a serviceman or servicewoman in many ways. Apart from their effect on his or her service career prospects, they could effect their career prospects in civilian life, and possibly their entitlement to a disability pension in the event of their discharge from the Army being recommended. In addition, the Boards' recommendation sometimes evoked an unfavourable reaction from an individual's CO, parents or some person in high office, which might lead to an appeal being made.

Patients' understanding of medical terminology at that time was increasing, and as a result, they had become aware of the implications of a condition, and the effects it might have on their way of life. Furthermore, there had been an increase in the frequency of negligence claims against doctors. Consequently, I had to give a good deal of thought and care to the way I conducted my Boards.

With regard to civilian candidates for entry to the Army, I had to consider the possibility of a condition deteriorating in the future, although not affecting his functional capacity at the time of his medical examination. Indeed, it was very important I bore in mind what the consequences might be if he broke down when leading a platoon or company on active service in the future. In addition, apart from taking into account the interest of the service and, indeed, the interests of the individual, I had to give due regard to the financial implications of the candidate being medically discharged during his basic training.

There were two particular conditions that sometimes caused my Board problems. One was epilepsy. The individual being recommended for discharge on the grounds that he suffered from recurrent seizures, invariably and for obvious reasons, strongly objected to the diagnosis of Epilepsy being recorded in the Boards Findings. On the other hand, the controversy that existed amongst clinicians, regarding the true nature, aetiology and management of M.E. (Myalgic Encephalomyelitis), made the Board unhappy about affirming the diagnosis in patients suffering from symptoms applicable to the condition, in the absence of any specific diagnostic tests being available. The patient by the time he would appear before us would have been seen by specialists in many different fields of medicine, and would have become firmly convinced that he was suffering from M.E. As a result, he would be very unhappy when we recommended that he should be discharged on the grounds that he suffered from the symptoms of Chronic Fatigue and Neurasthenia, which incidentally conformed with the *International Classification of Diseases*. From the field of new patterns of management of diseases, two heart and one heart/lung transplantation were presented to us for regarding of their fitness to perform their military duties. All these cases had recovered very well from their operations, and were physically quite fit, but of course were on long-term immuno-suppressive drug therapy. Both the heart transplant cases were discharged.

On the other hand, the heart/lung transplant case was found to have excellent functional capacity and motivation, and was deemed to be an exceptional case for retention, at least on a temporary basis and in a lowered medical category.

We had many casualties from the Falklands War and Northern Ireland referred to our Board for an assessment of their fitness to continue to undertake military duties. Incidentally, two of these cases were the subjects of television documentaries. These documentaries portrayed the progress of their recovery from their injuries from an early stage right up to and including their appearance at our Board. As President of the Board, it was my duty to inform these patients of the Findings of the Board, which in both cases was a recommendation that they should be medically discharged from the Army. On the day after one of these Boards was held, I was listening to the radio when I heard listeners phone in, and condemn me for being so uncaring and unjust when I recommended the serviceman's discharge from the Army. Later that day, when I went to pick up a daily paper from my newsagent, he stared at me, and then asked me to help him settle an argument he had had with his wife the previous night. She was adamant that she had seen me on television. He had disagreed with her. To re-establish cordial relations with his wife, I freely admitted that it was me she saw. I subsequently, made my way to a betting shop I sometimes visited. To my horror, as I stood at the counter, at the head of a long queue of 'customers', the lady behind the counter, in a loud voice exclaimed, 'I saw you on TV last night.' As a result, I was extremely embarrassed, having become an object of curiosity to all and sundry around me. Needless to say, I didn't set foot inside the shop again.

One dark winter's evening as I was about to drive home, I noticed that under my car, there was a milk bottle with a piece of a fabric in the bottom of it. I immediately thought that the object was highly suspicious of being something in the nature of a Molotov cocktail! I felt I needed a torch to examine it more closely, and proceeded to fetch one from the RSM's office. There, an Orderly was instructed to inspect the object with a strong light. The latter on making his inspection, exclaimed, 'What have we got here?', and immediately proceeded to pick the object up, exclaiming in a loud voice, 'It is a milk bottle.' Fortunately, it only contained a piece of an oily rag!

During this final phase of my career I took time off to return to Ireland and attend a wedding there. My son, Fergus, who was to be the best man at the wedding, accompanied me. We travelled to Rosslare by sea and then took a train from there to Dublin. This train journey turned out to be a hilarious experience. We understood that it would take only two hours for us to arrive in Dublin. It was going to be a fast journey. Little did we know what was in store for us. Soon after we started our journey, we stopped at small station where the guard proceeded to have a long conversation with the stationmaster. From then on we, for a while, continued to stop at every small station, and at each station the guard would have a chat with the stationmaster. Eventually, we began to think that we would be late for the wedding, and consequently, at the next station we told the guard that we had a wedding to attend and at the rate that we were travelling we would never get to it in time. His response was to tell us all about the wedding he attended recently and about what a lovely time he had. However, he did promise to 'speed things up'. To our horror, he was soon back to his old bad habits of conversing with the stationmaster when we stopped at a station. This time I put my arm out of our carriage door window and, to remind him of our predicament, pointed to my watch. His response was to inform me of the correct time! As time went on, he seemed to run short of stationmasters who were his friends, and we made up for some of our lost time. However, I regret to say there was to be one more hiccough on our journey. At a station outside Dublin, about five ticket inspectors got on board our train, and in their frantic efforts to complete their task before the train left the station, rushed up and down the train completely disorganised and falling over each other on one occasion. One inspector would have completed the operation in much less time. Having eventually arrived in Dublin, we hired a taxi to take us to our hotel. As we were in a great hurry to get to the wedding on time, I asked the taxi-driver to drive a bit faster. His response was to slow down and remark, 'Did you see that graveyard we have just passed? Well it is full of people like you, people who were always in a hurry, and look where they are now!' In the end, I am happy to say that we arrived in time for the wedding.

That taxi drive reminds me of another occasion when I was being driven in a taxi in Dublin. I was being driven from the airport into the City, when I became terrified by the reckless driving of my driver. I told him to slow down and drive more carefully. He related how he had been drinking too much recently, and that that very morning he had gone to a priest and signed the 'pledge'. Fortunately, he said, he had persuaded the priest to let him have the pledge on a temporary basis, and not for life, and as a result he could now stop at the next pub, and get himself sorted out. I managed to persuade him to continue our journey, and eventually drop me at my destination.

I found the work of a President of a Standing Medical Board so challenging, intriguing and rewarding, that I had to find a good reason for relinquishing the appointment. However, after being in the chair for ten years, I began to realise it was time I sat back and give some thought to finding the answer to Captain Boyles question, 'What is the stars?' I retired after reaching my seventieth birthday.

As I reach the end of this saga of my experiences of a doctor's life, I am mindful of the debt I owe to my parents, for the sacrifices they made to send me to university to study Medicine, and to my wife Eileen, for the unstinting support she gave me, and the loving care and guidance she gave to our children in the pursuit of their careers. Terence having studied at the LSE and London University became a political commentator on the radio and television. Fergus qualified as a doctor, having trained at the Westminster Hospital Medical School. Finola completed her nursing training at Charing Cross Hospital, and subsequently, initially, spent a considerable time working with a Medical Aid organization in Afghanistan refugee camps, and latterly as a Welfare Officer in the British Red Cross, serving in Northern Ireland, in the Gulf War, UK and Germany, Lastly, and not least, I am indebted to the late General Sir Alexander Drummond, who encouraged and motivated me to undertake a career in the Army Medical Services. I first met him during my National Service days in 1950 in Malaya, when he was the Senior Medical Officer (ADMS – Assistant Director of Medical Services). I soon came to admire his many fine qualities, and particularly his dynamism and his efficiency. Not many years later, he became Director General of the Army Medical Services. He was in my opinion the best DG the Corps ever had. During my service, he always took a great interest in my career, and was very kind to me. I remember my last meeting with him. He was in his eighties. I visited him when he was in hospital recovering from an operation. It so happened that at that time I was in need of a hair cut. As I was about to leave him, he turned to me and said, 'Pat, get your hair cut.' Then, as I walked away, he called me back, and remarked, 'Pat, you always seem to be dressed like an undertaker.' I smiled. He was quite right. I invariably wore a dark suit and dark overcoat!

As I left the hospital, I thought back to my first meeting with him, approximately thirty-five years ago, when he gave me an order to carry out, and now at what turned out to be our last meeting, he had again ordered me to do something, namely, to get my hair cut! To me, this latter incident, was a measure of our very amicable relationship.

Chapter 18

Postscript

After I retired, I found life away from the operating table, and the environment of the practice of medicine, at times, disturbing and difficult to cope with.

Soon after I retired, I played in a Veterans Cup competition at my golf club. The competition was held on a weekday, and as I had seldom played on a weekday, I knew very few of the members who were playing in it. Furthermore, I was ignorant of the fact that every competitor had to donate a bottle of wine or spirits to the prize fund, in order that every player would receive a prize of one of the aforementioned bottles. The person I was playing with, told me it would be in order for me to donate some golf balls in lieu of a bottle of wine or spirits. At the end of the competition, each player placed his bottle on a table in the room where the prizes were going to be presented. I had found two new golf balls in my golf bag, and having put them in an old packet I had found, I placed them on the table. As I, subsequently, walked back to my seat, to my horror, I could see on the faces of my fellow competitors as they gazed at the small object I had deposited on the table, looks of amazement and disbelief!

When the prize-giving commenced, I was pronounced the winner of the Cup. Later, when the time came for the person who came thirty-second and last in the competition to be presented with his prize, my little packet of golf balls, which was referred to as the booby prize, was presented to him. At the end of these proceedings, I was asked to make a speech; I felt my speech was good and appropriate to the occasion. Unfortunately, as I was finishing my speech, I could hear people in the audience muttering to one another that they hadn't heard a word I had said! All in all, I was not the most popular ever winner of the Cup. A year later, I was to go through the agony of believing I had had the Cup stolen from me. I brought the

Cup back to the club on the day before it was due to be competed for again. I left it in the locker room whilst I played a round of golf. Subsequently, when, I returned to the locker room, I found it had disappeared. That night, I couldn't sleep. I was thinking about the next morning, when I would have to inform the person who had donated the Cup, that I had lost his valuable trophy. However, fortunately, the next morning, I found it had all the time been in the safekeeping of the person in charge of the locker room. A year later, I received a phone call from the club reminding me not to forget to bring the Cup back for the competition being held the next day. I informed the caller that it was not me who had won the Cup in the previous year's competition, and that in fact, on that occasion I had lost the trophy on the day before the competition and then found it, and then lost it again on the day of the competition! The lesson I learnt from this cautionary tale, was, that, there must be more to life, than winning a cup playing golf!

One morning, I woke up feeling very happy and pleased with life. I was looking forward with great anticipation to buying a new car that day. Later when I sat down at the car salesman's desk, his greeting was, 'Nice to meet you Albert.' Throughout my career, I had always been called Patrick, my second Christian name, and I abhorred the name Albert, my first Christian name. Of course, the car salesman was not to know that. Nevertheless I was very irritated by his continued use of that name. Subsequently, I started to mention that I felt that this might be the last car I would ever buy, when he interrupted me, and said, 'I know what you are going to say. Albert you are under stress. Sit back and don't distress yourself. Relax Albert!' Later, as I walked out of the showroom, accompanied by him, and having bought a car from him, I proceeded to tell him why I preferred to be called Patrick, when he interrupted me again and said, 'Your very dear mother must have called you Albert.' I came away feeling no longer the cheerful and extroverted individual I was before I met my car salesman, and indeed felt I was in need of counselling by a social worker!

Epilogue

'Life is but a walking shadow, a poor player, that struts and frets his hour upon the stage, and is then heard no more.'

Shakespeare

FINIS.